LET'S SPEAK TWI

LET'S SPEAK TWI

A PROFICIENCY COURSE IN
AKAN LANGUAGE AND CULTURE

ADAMS BODOMO, CHARLES MARFO,
& LAUREN HALL-LEW

CSLI PUBLICATIONS

Center for the Study of
Language and Information
Stanford, California

Copyright © 2010
CSLI Publications
Center for the Study of Language and Information
Leland Stanford Junior University
Printed in the United States
14 13 12 11 10   1 2 3 4 5

Library of Congress Cataloging-in-Publication Data

Bodomo, Adams.
    Let's speak Twi : a proficiency course in Akan language and culture / Adams
Bodomo, Charles Marfo, and Lauren Hall-Lew.
      p. cm.
Text in English and Twi.
Includes bibliographical references.
ISBN 978-1-57586-604-8 (pbk. : alk. paper)
1. Twi language–Textbooks for foreign speakers–English.   I. Marfo, Charles.
II. Hall-Lew, Lauren. III. CSLI Publications (Firm) IV. Title.

PL8751.2.B63 2010
496′.338582421–dc22

2010017049
CIP

CSLI was founded in 1983 by researchers from Stanford University, SRI International, and Xerox
PARC to further the research and development of integrated theories of language, information, and
computation. CSLI headquarters and CSLI Publications are located on the campus of Stanford
University.

CSLI Publications reports new developments in the study of language,
information, and computation. Please visit our web site at
http://cslipublications.stanford.edu/
for comments on this and other titles, as well as for changes
and corrections by the author and publisher.

To Professor Will Leben, for promoting Ghanaian and African languages and linguistics in the United States, particularly at Stanford University.

To the Akan students at KNUST, Kumasi.

And in memory of Alberta "Sister-Afua" Ohenewah Shirley.

Contents

Introduction

This book, *Let's Speak Twi: A Proficiency Course in Akan Language and Culture*, is the outcome of many years of teaching and research on the Akan language and culture by the authors.

In September 2002, we started teaching at the University of Hong Kong (HKU), as part of a comprehensive research programme in African languages at the Department of Linguistics, a summer course and workshop in African Studies (SCOWAS). The main aim of the course was to create an atmosphere for graduate students and professors of Linguistics to elicit primary research materials on African languages and for students at the University of Hong Kong to learn an African language and culture, and this was indeed the first time that such a course was being offered anywhere in Hong Kong. The course and materials we produced were meant to be as naturalistic as possible based on and embedded in everyday African life in the rural areas of Africa where the language is used in its purest form.

Conversational Language Learning

In terms of language learning theories and frameworks, this book is based on the first author's theory of learning termed Conversational Learning Theory which highlights the important notion of *Conversational Learning Community* (CLC). CLC has been employed in the production of learning materials for languages such as Dagaare and Zhuang, the largest minority language spoken in China, and in the development of web-based materials for learning linguistics and related disciplines like Information Technology. This theory, as applied here, involves the creation of a sense of community among learners by gradually building up dialogues and activities based on everyday activities such greetings, introducing oneself, counting, making appointments, buying and selling things in the market, talking about the weather, giving directions, talking about family relations, eating and drinking, etc. The performance of these dialogues and the exercises associated with them are essential for creating a context in which learners use the language as if they were living everyday life as Akan people. New words and expressions are listed in each chapter to highlight them and to indicate when they first appeared. There is a more comprehensive Akan-English word list or abridged lexicon at the end of the book to serve as a handy reference for vocabulary acquisition. Grammatical points are not explicitly tabulated but the exercises form the basis for discussing these.

Orthographic Representation

Akan is a member of the Kwa branch of the Niger-Congo language family and it is mainly spoken in Ghana. It is encoded in the alphabetic writing system, which is well-established and widely used. However, it is important to note that, in documents written in Akan, some phonemes in the language are represented by different graphemes or alphabets from one author to the other. There are thirty-one graphemes including nine diagraphs in Akan: a, b, d, e, ɛ, f, g, h, i, k, l, m, n, o, ɔ, p, r, s, t, u, w, y, ky, gy, hy, tw, dw, ny, kw, hw, nw.

Akan is a two-tone language. The two tones are high (H) and low (L). H tone is indicated by the acute (') and L tone is indicated by the grave ('). The tones can sometimes be the only distinguishing factor between words (see (1)) and phrases (see (2)). In other words, tones could be lexically and grammatically significant in Akan. See *Appendix A* for more examples.

1. a. pápá   'goodness'
    b. pàpà   'fan'
    c. pàpá   'father'

2. a. Kòfi ńkásá   'Kofi should talk.'
    b. Kòfi ǹkásá   'Kofi does not talk'

Akan is a large language group with several regional varieties. The three most prominent are Asante Twi, Akuapem Twi, and Fante. This textbook mostly teaches Asante Twi forms, although Fante forms are sometimes given. Although the term Akan refers to all three varieties (as well as several others), throughout this text we use the terms 'Akan' and 'Twi' interchangeably, as people also often do in Ghana.

Acknowledgments

This book is result of many years of research into Akan language, culture, and society. We are very grateful to the University of Hong Kong and the Research Grants Council of Hong Kong for enthusiastically funding our research on Akan and other African languages through the RGC project number 10205398, the University Teaching Development Fund project number 10100188, and the KK Leung project numbers 21374047 and 21374058. The first author is very grateful to the second, who as doctoral candidate and later research assistant and tutor for the summer course on Twi, worked on many of his research projects involving Akan and other African languages.

   We are also grateful to members of the Linguistic Theory and Technology group who served as sounding boards for many issues on the structure of Akan first presented at our research meetings. We thank staff and students of the Faculty of Arts, especially those who have been taking our Summer Course in African Linguistics and Workshop in African Studies (SCOWAS), for their enthusiasm in participating in our research on Akan language and culture. Finally, we are grateful to all people who have read parts of this book and offered us crucial suggestions on how to improve it. We hope that learners of Akan and other users of this book will find it useful and we will be grateful for any feedback.

Adams Bodomo (Associate Professor, Hong Kong University, Hong Kong)
Charles Marfo (Lecturer, KNUST, Kumasi, Ghana)
Lauren Hall-Lew (Post-doctoral Fellow, University of Oxford, Oxford, UK)

1

Greetings & Other Phatic Expressions – *Ǹkyèá né Ǹsɛ́ḿ Bí*

When any person of the older generation (*i.e.*, grandmother, grandfather, mother, father, uncle, aunt, etc.) greets you, it is Akan custom to respond to that person as *father* or *mother*. Likewise, people in the older generation address members of the younger generation as their children when they respond to a greeting.

People in the same generation normally respond to each other as *brother* or *sister*. Also, depending on the relationship between the participants, one may respond to a greeting using phrases and words that indicate affection, feelings, or closeness, such as *my love*, *my world*, *my friend*, *my king*, etc.

Greetings are also typically paired with handshaking, but only among peers. Handshakes are rarely seen between people from different generations, except on special occasions. Examples of such occasions are i) where one of the parties has not been around for a long time (for instance, recently returned from a journey); ii) one party is congratulating the other on a particularly important achievement, etc. The right hand is used in handshaking and all other social situations that involve using the hands. It is considered impolite or insulting to use the left hand to greet or give something to another person, because the left hand is traditionally associated with taking care of things that are considered unclean.

1.1   Greetings – *ǹkyèá*

Derived phrase		Underlying phrase	Literal Meaning
Màdkyé	*Good Morning*	Mèmà wò àkyé.	'I wish you morning.'
Màdhá	*Good Afternoon*	Mèmà wò àhá.	'I give you light.'
Màdwó	*Good Evening*	Mèmà wò àdwó.	'I wish you coolness'
Ètè séń	*How are you?*	Wò ho tè séń?	'How is your body?'
Dùé / Yàákɔ̀	*Sorry (e.g., for your loss)*	Mèmà wò dùé. / Yàákɔ̀.	'I express sorrow.'
Wò tíńńkwá	*Good Luck*	Mèmà wò tíńkwá.	'I wish you luck.'
Nàntè yíé	*Farewell!*	Mèmà wò nàntè yíé.	'I wish you a good walk.'
Àfèhyìàpá	*Happy New Year*	Àfè ánó áhyíá pápá.	'The year has ended well.'

1.2   Responses – *ǹyèsɔ̀ɔ́*

Derived phrase		Underlying phrase	Literal Meaning
yàà / yɛ̀ɛ̀ ɛ̀nà	*good, mother*	Ɛ̀yɛ̀ ɛ̀ná.	'It is good, Mother'
yàà / yɛ̀ɛ̀ àgyà	*good, father*	Ɛ̀yɛ̀ àgyà.	'It is good, Father'
yàà/yɛ̀ɛ̀ nùá	*good, brother/sister*	Ɛ̀yɛ̀ ònùá.	'It is good, Brother/Sister'
yàà médɔ̀	*good, my love*	Ɛ̀yɛ̀ mé dɔ̀.	'It is good, my love'
yɛ̀ɛ̀ ɛ̀sɔ̀ń	*(A general response)*	Ɛ̀yɛ̀ ɛ̀sɔ́ń	'It is fine.' (general)
yàà mè bá / ɔ̀bá	*good, my child*	Ɛ̀yɛ̀ mè bá.	'It is good, my child.'
Ɛ̀yɛ̀	*It is fine/good.*	Mè hó yɛ́.	'My body is fine/good.'
Mèdààsè	*Thank you!*	Mèdà wó ásé.	'I lie under you.'
Àfé ńkɔ́ ḿmɛ́tó yɛ̀ǹ.	*May the year end well with us!*		'May the year come back to us'

1.3   A few helpful phrases for language learning – *Ǹsɛ́ḿ kàkrá bí á èhíá wɔ̀ kàsàsuá hó.*

Twi	English
Séń nà yɛ̀ká _____wɔ̀ Twì mú?	How do you say ____in Twi?
_____àsé né séń?	What does _____mean?
Mèǹté áseɛ́ɛ́ .	I don't understand.
Mèrèhyé àséɛ́ ásùá Twì.	I am starting to learn Twi.
Mèpààkyéw kàsá nyàà/bɔ̀kɔ̀ɔ̀.	Please speak slowly.
Mèpààkyéw tì dèɛ̀ wókáé nó mú bíó.	Please repeat what you said.
Wóbétúmí ásòpɛ́ɛ̀ nó?	Can you spell that?
Mèpààkyéw wóbétúmí átwèrɛ́ átò hɔ́?	Can you please write that down?
Mè wérè àfí!	I have forgotten!
Mèkàé!	I remember!

1.4 A few terms to note – *ǹsɛ̀mfùá bí à ɛ̀hó híá.*

Twi	English
àáné	yes
dààbí	no
àkwáàbà	welcome
mèpààkyɛ́ẃ	please / I beg you
dùé	sorry
bɔ̀kɔ̀ɔ́	calm / all right
kyèà	to greet
gyè só	to respond
ǹkɔ̀mmɔ́	conversation
kùróḿ	city centre
àsɔ́ré	church / chapel
àhìmfíé	palace
àfúó(ḿ)	farm
àfídíé / m̀fídíé	a trap / traps

Note that in Ghanaian English, which is often used intermixed with Akan, the phrase '*You are welcome*' is synonymous with the act of welcoming someone, rather than being something said after being thanked, as in other (e.g., United States) varieties of English.

1.5 Dialogues – *ǹkɔ̀mmɔ̀díé*

In the morning – *àno̖pá*

	Twi		English
Yàá:	Yàẁ, mèmà wò àkyé (màákyé)!	**Yaa:**	Yaw, good morning!
Yàẁ:	Yàà nùá! Nà wò hó tè sɛ̀n? (Nà ɛ̀té sɛ́ń)?	**Yaw:**	Good, brother. How are you?
Yàá:	Mèhò yɛ̀. / Ɛ̀yɛ̀. / Bɔ̀kɔ̀ɔ́.	**Yaa:**	I'm fine / it's fine / it's all right with me.
	Nà wó né àbùsùàfóɔ́ nó nyìnáá ńsóɛ̀?		What about you and the whole family?
Yàẁ:	Àà! Yɛ́ń nyìnáá hó yɛ́.	**Yaw:**	Well! We are all doing fine.
	Ná ɛ̀hé né àno̖pá yí? (Nà wórèkɔ́ héé àno̖pá yí?)		So where are you going this morning?
Yàá:	Mèrèkɔ̀hwɛ́ mè m̀fídíé.	**Yaa:**	I'm going to check on my traps.
	Mèrèkɔ̀té ànkàá.		I'm going to pluck oranges.
	Mèrèkɔ̀dí ńkɔ̀mmɔ́ bí.		I'm going to talk about some issue.
	Mèrèkɔ́àsɔ́ré.		I'm going to church.
	Nà wó ńsóɛ́?		What about you?
Yàẁ:	Mé ńsó mérèkɔ́ àfúóḿ / àhèm̀fíé / kùróḿ (ákɔ̀ hyìá ǹkr̀ɔ fóɔ́ bí).	**Yaw:**	I'm also going to the farm / the palace / town (to meet some people)

Yàá:	Yòò, ɛ́nèɛ̀ dùé né àwìá.	**Yaa:**	All right, then I sympathize you in the cold [i.e. I share your pain walking in a cold morning].
Yàẁ:	Mèdàasè. Kyèà òbíárá má mè.	**Yaw:**	Thank you. My regards to everyone.
	Yɛ̀bɛ́hyíá bíó.		We'll meet again.

In the afternoon – àwíá

	Twi		English
Yàẁ:	Màahá, mé núá!	**Yaw:**	Good afternoon, my brother!
Yàá:	Yàà nùá!	**Yaa:**	Good, brother!
	Wòfírì hé né àhópéré yí?		Where are you coming from in such a hurry?
	Wótùù kwáń ànáá?		Did you travel?
Yàẁ:	Àáné! Mèkɔɔ Kùmásí kɔdîi mé dwá bí.	**Yaw:**	Yes! I went to Kumasi for some business.
Yàá:	Àkwáàbà.	**Yaa:**	You are welcome back.
Yàẁ:	Mèdàasè. Nà m̀mòm̀ mésáń ákɔ ɔkyéná.	**Yaw:**	Thanks. But, I'll go back tomorrow.
Yàá:	Yòò! Ɛ́nnèɛ̀ dùé né òwìá.	**Yaa:**	All right! Then I sympathize with you in this sun (heat).
	Àféí ńsó, wó né Ònyàmé ńkɔ́.		Also, may God be with you.
Yàẁ:	Mèdàasè. Ɛ́nnèɛ̀, mɛ́hú wò àkyíré yí.	**Yaw:**	Thank you. Then, I will see you later.

Exercises

1. How would you greet someone during the following times of the day?

   a. In the evening: _____

   b. In the morning: _____

   c. In the afternoon: _____

2. How do you respond to the following people when they greet you?

    a.   Your mother   _____

    b.   Your uncle   _____

    c.   Your teacher   _____

    d.   Your sibling   _____

    e.   Someone of your age   _____

3. You have met your friend on your way to the town centre. Start a conversation with that friend, discussing his or her well-being, your well-being, and where each of you are going.

4. When greeting someone in Akan, which hand should be used? Why?

5. In the following dialogue box, fill in the gaps by answering the questions of your conversation partner, Attah.

		Twi		*English*
	Ata:	Mèmà wò àhá. / Màahá (mé núá).	**Attah:**	Good afternoon, (my brother/my sister).
i.	**Wo:**	_____.	**You:**	Good, brother!
	Ata:	Nà wò hó tè séń?	**Attah:**	How are you?
ii.	**Wo:**	_____.	**You:**	I am fine, thank you.
	Ata:	Ànɔpá yí dèè, wórèkɔ héé? Wórètù kwàǹ ánàà?	**Attah:**	Where are you going this morning? Are you travelling?
iii.	**Wo:**	_____.	**You:**	Yes! I am going to the farm. Is something the matter?
	Ata:	Dàabí. ɛnnèè ǹkyɛ́ bá.	**Attah:**	No. Then, don't keep long.
iv.	**Wo:**	_____.	**You:**	Alright! Thank you. I will see you this afternoon.

2

Twi Orthography – *Twi Àtwèrɛ́*

The standard Twi alphabetical system has 31 graphemes including 9 diagraphs. These graphemes comprise 24 consonants and 7 vowels. However, by the phenomenon of tongue root advancement with the vowels, technically known as Advance Tongue Root (ATR), there are three more graphemes. These three extra graphemes are variants of some vowels. In the following, these three graphemes are shown side by side with their counterparts. As also shown in the following, each grapheme is underlined in the example word(s).

	Graphemes	*In a word*	*Gloss*
1.	a / ɑ	ànòmàá / ɑ́dwúmá	bird / occupation
2.	b	báyíé	witchcraft
3.	d	dàdéɛ́	an iron
4.	e	dédé	noise
5.	ɛ	fɛ́rɛ́ɛ́	shyness
6.	f	afídíé	trap, machine
7.	g	gààrí	*a kind of food*
8.	h	àhìná	pot
9.	i / ɪ	sí / sɪ́	to wash / sharpen
10.	k	àkùmá	axe
11.	l	lɔ́ɔ́rì	lorry
12.	m	mààmé	woman
13.	n	nɛ̀téɛ́	soil
14.	o	dònnó	a kind of drum

6

15.	ɔ	sɔ̠ nèέ	sieve
16.	p	pánéέ	needle
17.	r	sɔ́r̠éέ	worship
18.	s	sàpɔ́	sponge
19.	t	tɪ̀tòmá	cloth
20.	u / ʊ	èb̠únúm / ɛ̀p̠ʊ́nʊ̠́	deep side / door, table
21.	w	wàdúró	mortar
22.	y	yàréέ	sickness
23.	ky	ɛ̀ky̠ɛ́	hat or cap
24.	gy [dʑ]	gyèéné	onion
25.	tw [tɕɥ]	tw̠ènéέ	drum
26.	dw [dʑɥ]	àdw̠éné	fish, brain
27.	ny [ɲ]	nyàmé	God or supreme being
28.	kw	ɛ̀kw̠áń	way
29.	hy [ɕ]	ɛ̀hyɛ́ń	brightness, transport
30.	hw [ɕɥ]	àhwèhwɛ́	mirror
31.	nw [ŋw]	nw̠únú	cold

Note: Pronouncing Akan-Twi correctly is more than just getting the vowels and consonants right. There are other important features of pronunciation that any learner must acquire to achieve full intelligibility and proficiency. These include attention to tones, nasalization patterns, and other phonological properties described in Appendix A.

Exercises

1. Practice saying the sounds of the Twi alphabet out loud with a partner, using the table above.

   (a) Can you write the letters that correspond to all the sounds? Try writing them without looking at the book.

   (b) Can you say all the sounds that correspond to all the letters? Practice saying the letters as your teacher or partner writes them on the blackboard.

2. Practice saying the Twi words in which these sounds appear.

3. Refer to Appendix A, and practice saying aloud some of the more advanced pronunciation features, such as vowel harmony, contrasting tones, and contrasting nasalization patterns. Be sure to practice these differences with the aid of a native speaker!

3

Introducing Oneself – *Òbí Réyí Nò Hó Ádíé*

3.1 Pronouns – *èdíń ńsíànáámú*

Personal Pronouns

In Twi, unlike in English, the form of a personal pronoun is the same in the subject and the object positions, as shown in the table below. Observe in the table that the third person singular pronoun is normally represented in the subject position with the initial syllables, /ɔ/ and /ɛ/ (for animate and inanimate nouns respectively). Also observe that, in the object position, the last syllable, *no*, is normally used.

Person	Subject		Object	
	Singular	*Plural*	*Singular*	*Plural*
1st	mé	yέ(ń)	mè	yὲǹ
	I	*we*	*me*	*us*
2nd	wó	mó	wò	mò
	you	*you*	*you*	*you*
3rd	ɔ̀(nó) ὲ(nò)	wɔ́ń	(ɔ̀)nó (ὲ)nó	wɔ̀ǹ
	she/he it	*they*	*her/him it*	*them*

Note that the third person singular shows no gender (i.e. male-female) distinction. In the following, each of the pronouns is used in a sentence, as a subject and an object.

    a. <u>Mè</u>-tàǹ <u>wò</u>.   'I hate you.'
    b. <u>Wó</u>-tàǹ <u>mè</u>.   'You hate me.'
    c. <u>Ɔ̀</u>-dɔ̀ <u>wɔ̀ń</u>.   'She/he loves them.'
    d. <u>Ὲ</u>-wòsó.   'It shakes.'
    e. <u>Ma</u>-bú <u>nò</u>.   'I've broken it.' / 'I've cheated him/her.'
    f. <u>Yὲ</u>-dɔ̀ <u>mò</u>.   'We love you.'
    g. <u>Mó</u>-dɔ̀ <u>yὲǹ</u>.   'You love us.'
    h. <u>Wɔ̀ń</u>-dɔ̀ <u>nó</u>.   'They like her/him.'

Possessive Pronouns

When any of the personal pronouns is put before a noun, it becomes a possessive pronoun. In other words, as shown below, the pronouns do not change in form in the possessive forms.

a.	Mé + ɛ̀dáń	→ Mé dáń	'my house'
b.	Wó + ètúó	→ Wó túó	'your gun'
c.	Ɔ̀nó + ètúó	→ Nó/né túó	'her/his/its gun'
d.	Yɛ̀ń + ɛ̀dáń	→ Yɛ̀(ń) dáń	'our house'
e.	Mó + sìká	→ Mó sìká	'your money'
f.	Wɔ́ń+ pàpá	→ Wɔ́ń pàpá	'their father'

Interrogative Pronouns

The following are also the interrogative pronouns in Twi. As shown in examples (a–f), observe that each of the pronouns is a substitute of a noun or a phrase.

déɛ́ń, déɛ́ bɛ́n	'what/which, what thing'
hwáń / hwáánóḿ	'who (singular / plural)
sɛ́ń	'how / how much'
dódóɔ́ sɛ́ń	'how many'
ɛ̀hé / ɛ̀héfá	'where / which place'
dà bɛ́ń / bɛ́ɛ́ bɛ́n	'when / what time'
(sɛ́) ádɛ́ń / (sɛ́) ádɛ́ń ńtí	'why / for what reason'

Examples:

	Statement			*Interrogative*	
a.	Wópɛ̀ sìká.	'You like money.'	→	Wópɛ̀ déɛ́n?	'What do you like?'
b.	Wódɔ̀ Kòfì.	'You love Kofi.	→	Wódɔ̀ hwáń?	'Who do you like?"
c.	Mèhìá dú.	'I need ten.'	→	Méhíá sɛ́ń?	'How many do I need?'
d.	Òkòò fíé.	'He went home.'	→	Ɔ̀kɔ̀ɔ̀ héfá?	'Where did he go?'
e.	Mɛ́bá ǹnɛ̀ .	'I'll come today.'	→	Mɛ́bá dàbɛ́ń?	'When will I come?'
f.	Ɔ̀àséré sɛ́ Kòfí ákà àsèrésɛ́ḿ.	'She laughed because Kofi told a joke.'	→	Ɔ̀àséré sɛ́ déɛ́ń?	'She has laughed for what reason (why has she laughed?)'

Demonstrative Pronouns

The following are the demonstrative pronouns in Twi. As also shown below, they come after the nouns they demonstrate.

Twi	English	Twi	English
yèí / wèí	'this (one)'	pàpá yèí / wèí	'this man'
ɔ̀nó	'that (one)' [human]	pàpá (ɔ̀)nó	'that man'
ɛ̀nó	'that (one)' [non-human]	ɛ̀dáń (ɛ̀)nó	'that house'
yèínóḿ / wèínóḿ	} 'these (ones)'	àtúó yèí(nóḿ)	} 'these (guns)'
sàá ... yí		sàá átúó yí	
sàá ... nó	'those (ones)'	sàá ńsàfòà nó	'those keys'

3.2 Asking one's name – *èdíń bísá*

Type 1:

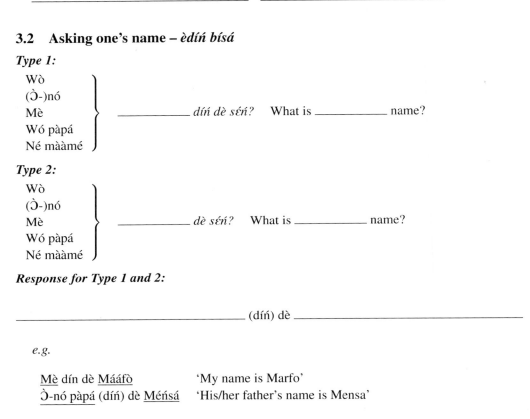

Wò
(Ɔ̀-)nó
Mè
Wó pàpá
Né mààmé
} _____ *díń dè sɛ́ń?* What is _____ name?

Type 2:

Wò
(Ɔ̀-)nó
Mè
Wó pàpá
Né mààmé
} _____ *dè sɛ́ń?* What is _____ name?

Response for Type 1 and 2:

_____ (díń) dè _____

e.g.

Mè dín dè Mááfò 'My name is Marfo'
Ɔ̀-nó pàpá (díń) dè Méńsá 'His/her father's name is Mensa'

Type 3:

Yefre { Wò / (Ɔ̀-)nó / Mè / Wó pàpá / Né mààmé } *sen* What is ____ name (what do we call ____)?

Response for Type 3:

Yɛ̀fɾɛ́ _____

e.g.

Yɛ̀fɾɛ́ <u>mè</u> <u>Mááfɔ̀</u>	'My name is Marfo'
Yɛ̀fɾɛ́ <u>yɛ́ń</u> <u>pàpá</u> <u>Méńsá</u>	'Our father's name is Mensa'

3.3 A dialogue about introducing oneself – *Ǹkɔ̀m̀mɔ́ bí à ɛ̀fá òbí réyí nò hó ádíé hó*

	Twi		English
Mà,àmé:	Mè bá, yɛ̀fɾɛ́ wò sɛ́ń? (Wò díń dè sɛ́ń?)	**Woman:**	My son, what is your name?
Yàẁ:	Yɛ̀fɾɛ́ <u>mè</u> Yàẁ Àtá. (Mè díń dè Yàẁ Àtá.)	**Yaw:**	My name is Yaw Attah.
Mà,àmé:	Nà w'àwófóɔ́ ńsóɛ́.	**Woman:**	What about your parents?
Yàẁ:	Mè pàpá díń dè Òwúrà Kwà, àkú Òwúsú, ɛ́nà yɛ̀fɾɛ́ mé màà mé ńsó Òwúràyéré Àfíá Òwúsú.	**Yaw:**	My father's name is Mr. Kwaku Owusu, and my mother is (also) called Mrs. Afua Owusu.
Mà, àmé:	Mófɾì héfà?	**Woman:**	Where do you come from?
Yàẁ:	Yɛ̀fɾì Bɛ̀kwáɛ̀ áà ɛ̀wɔ́ Àsàntɛ́ máńtám̀ mú. Nàńsó sèèsɛ̂ì déɛ́, yɛ̀tè Àsàfò, Kùmáseé.	**Yaw:**	We come from Bekwai, which is in the Asante region. However, at the moment, we live at Asafo, Kumasi.
Mà, àmé:	W'ànó átè páá. Wókɔ́ sùkúù ànáá?	**Woman:**	You're very eloquent. Do you go to school?
Yàẁ:	Àáné mèyɛ̀ sùkúùní.	**Yaw:**	Yes, I'm a student.
Mà, àmé:	Kà wò hó àsɛ́m̀ kàkɾá ká hó kyérɛ̀ mè.	**Woman:**	Tell me a little more about yourself.
Yàẁ:	Yòò! M'àdí m̀féɛ́ àdùɔ̀nù. Mèkɔ́ sùkúù wɔ́ Gáánà Sùkúùpɔ̀ǹ mú. Mèǹwáréɛ̀ɛ̀, nàńsó mèwɔ̀ m̀pénà. Àgórɔ́ á mèpɛ́ né bɔ́ɔ̀lò bɔ́, ɛ́nà àdùàné á mèpɛ́ né ɛ̀mó né àdùà. Mèká Twì ne Ɛ́ngèlésì bɾɔ̀fó. Ɛ̀yɛ́ mè sɛ́ mè hó ásɛ́m̀ nyìnáá né nó.	**Yaw:**	Alright! I'm twenty years old. I attend school at the University of Ghana. I'm not married, but I've a girl-friend. The game I like best is football/soccer, and the food I like best is rice with beans. I speak Twi and English. It looks like that is about all (about me).

Mà:àmé:	Ǹtì wóńyɛ́ ádwúmá bíáɾá?		**Woman:**	So, don't you have any job?
Yàẁ:	Dààbí! Nàńsó, àkwámá mú nó, mèbòá m'áwófóɔ́ wɔ́ àfúó mú.		**Yaw:**	No! But, during vacations, I help my parents in the farm.
Mà:àmé:	Yòò ńtí ɛ̀kyèɾɛ́ sɛ́ w'àwófóɔ́ yɛ̀ àkùàfóɔ́?		**Woman:**	Alright, does that mean your parents are farmers?
Yàẁ:	Àáné! Màká mè hó ásɛ́m̀ pìì àkyéɾɛ́ wó. Wó ńsó ká bìrìbí fá wó hó kyérɛ̀ mè.		**Yaw:**	Yes! I've told you a lot about myself. You should also tell me something about yourself.
Mà:àmé:	Mɛ́yɛ́ sàá dà fófóɾɔ́ áà yèbéhyíá bíó.		**Woman:**	I'll do that the next time we meet again.

Exercises

1. Memorise the various *personal pronouns* in Akan and practice their pronunciation.

2. Practice using the personal pronouns in class with your tutor, teacher, or classmates, using the dialogue in this chapter as your model.

3. Acting like it's the first day of class, tell your new classmates various things about yourself, without referring to the textbook.

4. Substitute each of the underlined words in the following statements with the appropriate *interrogative pronoun* in Twi and read your answers to your classmates.

	Statement		*Interrogative*
e.g.,	<u>Kòfí</u> ábà fíé.	'Kofi has come home.'	<u>*Hwan*</u> na aba fie.
a.	Kòfí ábà <u>fíé</u>	'Kofie has come home.'	_____
b.	Wóábɔ̀ <u>Kòfí</u>	'You have hit Kofi.'	_____
c.	<u>Mèpɛ̀</u> ǹtɛ́ mmìènú.	'I want two marbles.'	_____
d.	Mèpɛ̀ ǹtɛ́ <u>mmìènú.</u>	'I want two marbles.'	_____
e.	ɔ̀bɛ́dá há <u>kyéná</u>	'She/he will sleep here tomorrow.'	_____

5. Which Twi *pronouns* represent the underlined words in the following sentences?

    (a) <u>Kòfí</u> kɔ́ <u>àfúó mú</u>. ('Kofi goes to farm.') : _____kɔ́ _____.

    (b) <u>Kòfí né Àdú</u> ábóá <u>Ámá</u>. ('Kofi and Adu have helped Ama.') :

    _____ábóá _____.

4

Numerals – *Ǹkóńtá / Àkòǹtàbúdéɛ́*

	English	Twi
1	one	ɛ̀kó, bààkó
2	two	m̀mìènú
3	three	m̀mìènsá
4	four	(ɛ̀)náń
5	five	(è)núḿ
6	six	(è)ǹsìá
7	seven	(è)ǹsóń
8	eight	nwɔ̀twé
9	nine	(ɛ̀)ǹkŕóń
10	ten	(è)dú
11	eleven	dúbààkó
12	twelve	dú m̀mìènú
20	twenty	àdùònú
21	twenty-one	àdùònú bààkó
22	twenty-two	àdùònú m̀mìènú
30	thirty	àdùàsà
31	thirty-one	àdùàsà bààkó
32	thirty-two	àdùàsà m̀mìènú
40	forty	àdùànáń
41	forty-one	àdùànáń bààkó

42	forty-two	àdùànáń m̀mìènú
50	fifty	àdùònúḿ
51	fifty-one	àdùònúḿ bààkó
52	fifty-two	àdùònúḿ m̀mìènú
60	sixty	àdùòsíá
61	sixty-one	àdùòsíá bààkó
62	sixty-two	àdùòsíá m̀mìènú
70	seventy	àdùɔsóń
71	seventy-one	àdùɔsóń bààkó
72	seventy-two	àdùɔsóń m̀mìènú
80	eighty	àdùɔwɔ́twé
81	eighty-one	àdùɔwɔ́twé bààkó
82	eighty-two	àdùɔwɔ́twé m̀mìènú
90	ninety	àdùɔkŕóń
91	ninety-one	àdùɔkŕóń bààkó
92	ninety-two	àdùɔkŕóń m̀mìènú
100	one hundred	ɔhà
101	one hundred one	ɔhà né kó / bààkó
102	one hundred two	ɔhà nè m̀mìènú
110	one hundred ten	ɔhà nè dú
200	two hundred	àhàànú
201	two hundred one	àhàànú né bààkó
202	two hundred two	àhàànú né m̀mìènú
211	two hundred eleven	àhàànú né dúbààkó
220	two hundred twenty	àhàànú né àdùònú
300	three hundred	àhààsà
400	four hundred	àhánáń
500	five hundred	àhánúḿ
1,000	one thousand	àpéḿ
2,000	two thousand	m̀péḿ m̀mìènú
3,001	three thousand one	m̀péḿ m̀mèɛ̀nsá né bààkó
1,000,000	one million	ɔpèpéḿ
1,000,000,000	one billion	ɔpèpè péè

4.1 A dialogue about numerals – Ǹkɔmmɔ́díe bí à ɛ̀fá ǹkóńtá hó

	Twi		English
Àfúá:	Yàẁ, wóádì m̀féɛ́ sɛ́ń?	**Afua:**	Yaw, how old are you?
Yàẁ:	Màdí m̀féɛ́ àdùònúmìènú.	**Yaw:**	I'm twenty-two years old.
Àfúá:	Kúmá, wó ńsóɛ́?	**Afua:**	Kumah, what about you?
Kúmá:	Mé ńsó m'ádì dúnwótwé. Ádéń nà wórébísá?	**Kumah:**	I'm also eighteen (as for me, I'm 18). Why are you asking?

Àfúá:	Sὲέ móyὲ ǹkwàdàá. Yὲká mó míènú ḿfíé bóḿ ḿpó áà ǹnú mé dèέ.	**Afua:**	Then you are just children. If we combine the years of both of you they do not add up to mine.
Yàẁ:	Mèǹnyé ǹní. Ká kyérὲ yὲǹ. Wóádì ḿféέ sέń?	**Yaw:**	I don't believe it. Tell us. How old are you?
Àfúá:	Màdí àdùànáńḿmìènú.	**Afua:**	I'm forty-two.
Kúmá:	Éì! έnèὲ sέ àká kàkŕá bí nà wó né mé màámé pέ.	**Kumah:**	Ai! Then you're almost the same age as my mother.
Àfúá:	Sàá á? Wó màámé wɔ ḿféέ sέń?	**Afua:**	Is that so? How many years does your mother have (how old is your mother?)
Kúmá:	Ɔwɔ ḿféέ ádùànáńnàǹ pέ.	**Kumah:**	She is only forty-four years old.
Yàẁ:	Sàá á? Ńsó ɔsὲ òbí áà ɔádí béyέ ḿféέ ádùònúḿ rékɔ nó.	**Yaw:**	Is that so? But she looks like someone who is fifty years or more.
Kúmá:	Ṁmáá né nó! Wòyíní gyá wɔn ḿfíé hɔ. Mé pàpá ná ɔàyíní páá. Ɔàdí ḿféέ àdùònúḿnúḿ.	**Kumah:**	That is the case with women! They grow faster than their age. It is my father who is very old. He is fifty-five years old.
Àfúá:	Énèὲ nò hó nà ὲyέ fέ. Ɔǹsέ òbí áà ɔàdí sàá.	**Afua:**	Then he is just handsome. He doesn't look like someone who is that age.

4.2 A dialogue about numerals – Ǹkɔmmɔdíe bí à ὲfá ǹkóńtá hó

	Twi		*English*
Sàr̀fó:	Yàẁ, wó pàpá ńkóɔ yέ sέń?	**Sarfo:**	Yaw, how many chickens does your father have?
Yàẁ:	Ɔwɔ ńkókɔ ḿmèέǹsá, òniní bààkó nà àbédéέ ḿmìènú. Mó ńsó mówɔ sέń?	**Yaw:**	He has three chickens: one cock and two hens. How many do you also have? (As for you, how many do you have?)
Sàr̀fó:	Mà méńhwέ. Mègyé dí sὲ yèwɔ bὲyὲ dúnúḿ.	**Sarfo:**	Let me see. I believe we have about fifteen of them.
Kúmá:	Éí! Énèὲ móáyὲ àdéέ. Nà ǹnwáń né ḿpòǹkyé ńsóέ?	**Kumah:**	Ai! Then you have done well. What about sheep and goats?
Sàr̀fó:	Yὲwɔ ǹnwáń ǹnúḿ, έnà ḿpɔǹkyé ńsón.	**Sarfo:**	We have five sheep and, also, seven goats.
Yàẁ:	Ǹtì, yὲká wón nyìnáá bóḿ áà mówɔ àyέḿmóá dúmìènú. Énèὲ yὲwɔ dódó sén mò.	**Yaw:**	So, if we add them up you have twelve livestock. Then we have more than you.
Kúmá:	Sàá á? Mówɔ dódóɔ sέń?	**Kumah:**	Is that so? How many do you have?

Yàẁ:	Yɛ̀wɔ̀ ǹnwáń ńkŕóń nà m̀pòǹkyé ǹsó dúbààkó.	**Yaw:**	We have nine sheep and eleven goats.

Exercises

1. Tell your friends how old you are in Twi. (*e.g., Màdí m̀féɛ̀ ... / mèwɔ̀ m̀féɛ́ ...*)

2. In Twi:

   (a) Tell your friends the number of people in your family.

   (b) Tell your friends how old each of them is. (*e.g., Mè pàpá ádì m̀féɛ̀ ....*)

3. Try to count (by saying aloud) the people or tables in your class in Twi.

4. In the following number table, fill in the gaps with the appropriate Twi numbers:

	20 àdùònù	30 àdùàsà	40 àdùànán	50 àdùònúm	60 àdùòsíá	70 àdùòsón	80 àdùòwótwé	90 dùòkrón	100 óhà
1 bàakó	àdùònú-bàakó								
2 mìènú						àdùòsón-mìènú			
3 ǹmèènsá	àdùònù-ǹmèènsá				àdùòsíá-ǹmèènsá				
4 ènán		àdùàsànán							
5 ènúm			àdùànán-núm						
6 ǹsíá									
7 ènsón					àdùòsíá-ńsón				
8 nwòtwé						àdùòsón-nwòtwé			
9 ǹkrón									

Telling Time: Days of the Week & Months of the Year – *Ṁmrɛ́ kà, Ǹná á ɛ̀wɔ́ nàwɔ́twé mú, Àbòsómé á ɛ̀wɔ́ àfé mú*

In the olden days of the Asante, Akuapem and Fante societies, bells (*ɛ̀dɔ́ń* in Twi) were rung at every hour to tell people the time of day. This symbolic chiming of the bell has been a major reference to the way that telling time is expressed in Akan. The following table shows how Twi speakers refer to particular points in time.

Twi	Number	English
sìm̀má / sìm̀má bààkó	1 min.	a minute / one minute
dɔ̀nhwérè / dɔ̀nhwérè bààkó	1 hr.	an hour / one hour
àhòmàkyé dɔ́ńkó né fá	1:30 a.m.	half past one in the early morning (dawn)

Twi	Number	English
àhòmàkyé ǹnɔ́ń núḿ	5 a.m.	five o'clock in the early morning (dawn)
ànɔpá ǹnɔ́ń ǹsíá	6 a.m.	six o'clock in the morning
ànɔpá ǹnɔ́ń dú	10 a.m.	ten o'clock in the morning
àwìá dú m̀mìènú / p̀rɛ̀mòtóbŕɛ́	12 p.m.	noon / 'canon-blasting-time'
àwìá dɔ́ń kò	1 p.m.	one o'clock in the afternoon
ànwùmérɛ́ ǹnɔ̀ǹ náń	4 p.m.	four o'clock in the afternoon
ànàdwó ǹnɔ̀ǹ dú	10 p.m.	ten o'clock in the night
ànàdwó dú m̀mìènú	12 a.m.	midnight
ǹnɔ́ń m̀mèɛ̀nsá né fá / ǹnɔ́ń m̀mèɛ̀nsá ápáé mú	3:30	half past three (either dawn or afternoon)
dɔ̀ń kó ápà hó sìmá dú núḿ	1:15	a quarter past one (either dawn or afternoon)
Àká sìm̀má dú núḿ ná àbɔ́ ǹnɔ́ń m̀mìènú.	It's 1:45	It is a quarter to two (either dawn or afternoon).
Ǹnɔ́ń m̀mìènú ápà hó sìmá ádùàsá núḿ.	It's 2:35.	It is thirty-five minutes past two.
Àká sìm̀má ádúònú núḿ ná àbɔ́ ǹnɔ́ń m̀mèɛ̀nsá.	It's 2:35.	It is twenty-five minutes to three.

5.1   Some expressions of time – *m̀mérɛ́ mú ńkèkàéɛ́ bí*

Twi	English
ɛ̀bérɛ́	time
àhòmàkyé	dawn
ànɔpá	morning
àwìá	afternoon
ànwùmérɛ́ (nwúnú + bérɛ́)	evening (cool + time)
ànàdwó	night
ànàdwó bérɛ́	night time
àwìá bérɛ́	day time / afternoon
ànàdwó dàsúó mú	deep in the night
Yɛ̀kɔ́ àdwúmá (ànɔpá) ǹnɔ̀ǹ ǹsóń né fá.	We go to work at 7:30 a.m.
Yɛ̀pɔ́ń àdwúmá áká sìm̀má dú ámá ábɔ́ ànwùmérɛ́ ǹnɔ̀ǹ núḿ.	We close from work at 10 minutes to 5 p.m.
Àbɔ̀ ǹnɔ̀ǹ náń ápàhó mínìtì dú.	The clock is 10 minutes after 4 o'clock.
Sɛ̀ ɛ̀ká sìm̀má dúnúḿ ámà bɔ̀ ǹnɔ̀ǹ núḿ áà nyàè mè.	When it is quarter to five, wake me up.

Kétékyé nó bɛ́bá ábɛ̀dú ànàdwó dú m̀mìènú m̀páèmú (em i.e., dú m̀mìènú né fá).	The train will arrive at 12:30 a.m.
Wìèmhyɛ́n nó bɛ́kɔ́ ákɔ̀dú Àméríkà ɔkyéná ànɔpá ǹnɔ̀ǹ ǹsíá ápá hó dú m̀mìènú.	The aeroplane will arrive in America at 6:12 a.m.
Ǹnɔ̀ǹ ǹkrón pépɛ́ɛ́pɛ́ ná m̀mɔ̀frá ńkétéwá nó nyìnáá ádédá.	At exactly 9:00, all the little children will be asleep.
Kòfí dí ànwùmérɛ́ ádúàné ǹnɔn ǹwɔtwé.	Kofi eats dinner at eight o'clock.
Ǹsúó átɔ̀ átóá só ǹnɔ̀nhwéré m̀mɛ̀ɛnsá.	It has rained continuously for three hours.
Mèdá ànàdwó ńnɔ́ń dú ná màsɔ́ré ánɔpá ǹnɔ̀ǹ ǹsóń né fá.	I go to bed at ten o'clock in the night and wake up at half past seven in the morning.
Àhòmàkyé ǹnɔ̀ǹ núm̀ bíárá, mèbɔ́ m̀páé.	At five o'clock each dawn, I pray.

5.2 Day of the week – *Ǹná à ɛ̀wɔ́ nàwɔ́twé mú*

Akan culture has seven days in a week, just as in English. Among the Akans (Asantes, Fantes and Akuapems), the day one is born automatically becomes the basis of one's name. These day-associated names are called *dàdíń* day names', as shown below with gender distinction:

Asante-Twi	English		Male Name	Female Name
Kwàsíádá	Sunday	:	Àkwàsí	Àkósúá
Ɛ̀dwóádá	Monday	:	Kwàdwó	Àdwóá
Ɛ́bénádá	Tuesday	:	Kwàbèná	Àbénáá
Wùkúádá	Wednesday	:	Kwàkú	Àkúá
Yáwóádá	Thursday	:	Yàẁ	Yàá
Èfíádá	Friday	:	Kòfí	Àfúá
Méménédá	Saturday	:	Kwámè	Àmá

5.3 Months of the year – *Àbòsómè à ɛ̀wɔ́ àfé mú*

Again, just like in English-speaking cultures, Akan culture has twelve months in a year. As listed below, the names associated with the months are derived in one of the following ways:

1. Some months are named according to their places or positions in the ordering of the months.
2. Some others are named after a unique weather condition in these particular months.
3. The names of others are based on occurrences in the life of people in these particular months.

So, the name of each month has its own particular meaning. But these days, it is common to find speakers of Akan using the English forms, instead.

Twi	English
Ɔbɛpɔ́n	January
Ɔgyèfóɔ	February
Òbèním	March
Òfòrísúó	April
Òkòtònímáá	May
Àyɛ́wòhómɔ́bɔ́	June
Kìtàwònsá	July
Ɔsànàá	August
Ɛbɔ́	September
Àhínìmè	October
Òbúbúó	November
Òpènímmáá / Br̀ònyà bòsómé	December / Christmas month

5.4 Some expressions with days of the week and months of the year – *Ǹsɛ́m bí á ɛ̀fá ǹná à ɛ̀wɔ́ ǹnàwɔ́twé mú né àbòsómè à ɛ̀wɔ́ àfé mú hó*

Twi	English
Yɛ̀wòò mè Wùkúádá, ńtí mè díń dè Kwàkú (ɔ̀bàrímá). / Àkúá. (ɔ̀báá)	I was born on Wednesday, so I am called Kwaku. (male) / Akua. (female).
Yɛ̀wòò Kòfí Òfòrísúó dá áà ɛ̀tɔ́ só dúnáń mú, àfé m̀pím mìènú mú.	Kofi was born on the 14th of April, in the year 2000.
Yɛ̀dí búròyà wɔ̀ bòsómé Òpènímmáá mú.	We celebrate Christmas in the month of December.
Gááná nyàà fàahódíé wɔ̀ Òbèním dá á ɛ̀tɔ́ sò ńsìá mú, wɔ̀ àfé àpím àhá ńkrón ádùònúḿ ńsóń mú.	Ghana gained independence on the 6th of March 1957.
Ǹsúó tɔ́ kɛ̀sɛ́ɛ́ páá wɔ̀ àbòsómé Àyɛ́wòhómɔ́bɔ́ né Kìtàwònsá mú.	It rains a lot in June and July.
Ɔgyèfóɔ dá áà ɛ̀tɔ́ só dúnán wɔ̀ àfé bíárá mú yɛ̀ *Valentine* (àdɔ́fóɔ́) dá.	The 14th of February of every year is Valentine's (lovers') Day.

5.5 A dialogue based on days of the week and months of the year – *Ǹsέḿ bí à èfá ǹná à ὲwɔ ǹnàwɔ́twé mú né àbòsómè à ὲwɔ àfé mú hó*

	Twi		English
Ákú:	Kòfí, dà béń nà wò yéré béwó?	**Aku:**	Kofi, when (on which day) will your wife deliver (her baby)?
Kòfí:	Òbéwó Àyέwòhómɔbɔ dá áà ὲtɔ sò dú ńsóń, ǹsò èbíà έńnú sàá.	**Kofi:**	She will deliver on the 17th day of June, but it may not be that long.
Ákú:	Àdέń nà wóréká sàá? Bìrìbí ákɔ bɔné ànáá?	**Aku:**	Why are you saying that? Is something wrong?
Kòfí:	Mèkɔ húù òdùyέfóɔ ǹnànsá né ńnέ, nà ɔkyèré sέ èbíà Yàá béwó ńtέḿ.	**Kofi:**	I went to see a doctor three days ago, and he explained that, maybe, Yaa would deliver early.
	Èfrì sέ àbòfrá nò kèká nè hò páá.		This is because the child is kicking too much.
Ákú:	Yòò.	**Aku:**	Alright.
	Ὲyέ áà sὲ Yàá sέ ɔ́ńkáé sέ yὲbéhyíá Yáwóádá ádì Méménédá áyíé nó hó ńkɔ̀ḿmɔ́, ànídíé mú.		Tell Yaa that she should remember that we will meet this Thursday to talk about the funeral on Saturday, please.
Kòfí:	Ὲǹyέ hwὲὲ, mέká ákyèrέ nó. Nà, hwáń áyíé né nó?	**Kofi:**	It is nothing (at all), I will tell her. So, whose funeral is it?
Ákú:	Éi! Nà wó dèὲ wóńté kùróḿ há? Kòó Nìmó áwú béyέ bòsómé náń ní yí. Wóńtéὲὲ?	**Aku:**	Ei! Are you not living in this town? It is about four months ago that Koo Nimo died. Haven't you heard?
Kòfí:	Óò! Mènníḿ. Wónìm sέ, m'àdwúmá yí, mèkɔ Ὲdwóádá áà, mèbá Èfíádá ánwùmérέ. Έńtí mèntè dèὲ ὲrékɔ sò bíárá.	**Kofi:**	Oh! I didn't know that. You know that, with my work, if I go on Monday, I come back on Friday evening. So, I don't hear of whatever is going on.
Ákú:	Ὲyὲ nòkwárέ. Έnèὲ mèrèkɔ́, Ὲsὲ sέ mèhyíá mé kúnú dɔ́ń kó né fá. Yὲbéhyíá bíó.	**Aku:**	It is true. Then I'm going, I have to meet my husband at 1:30. We will meet again.
Kòfí:	Yòò! Nàntè yíé, wó né Nyàmé ńkɔ.	**Kofi:**	Alright! Have a good day, may God be with you.
	Ὲyé áà kyὲà wó kúnú má mè.		My regards to your husband.

Exercises

1. In the following, write the Twi sentences that correspond to the English sentences:

	Twi	*English*
a.	Àbɔ̀ àhòmàkyé dɔ́ń kó.	It is one o'clock in the early morning.
b.	_____	It is fifteen minutes past two o'clock in the afternoon.
c.	_____	It is a quarter to five o'clock in the evening.
d.	_____	I wake up at six o'clock in the early morning.
e.	_____	He was born around ten o'clock at night.
f.	_____	I eat lunch at exactly twelve noon / 'canon-blasting-time'.
g.	_____	My father comes home from work at twenty-five minutes past seven from Monday to Friday.

2. Without looking back at the book, try saying the Akan names for men and women born on:
    - (a) Tuesday
    - (b) Friday
    - (c) Sunday
    - (d) Thursday
    - (e) Saturday
    - (f) Monday
    - (g) Wednesday

3. Tell your friends on which day and in which month you were born.
    e.g., *Yèwòò mè Èbɔ́ dá áà ètɔ́ sò dú ńsìà*
    'I was born on (the) 16th (day of) September.'

4. Use this website http://www.onlineconversion.com/dayborn.htm or use http://www.google.com to determine what day of the week you were born on, if you don't already know. Then tell your classmates your Akan name (e.g., *Mè díń dè ...* or *Yɛ̀frɛ́ mè ...*). As an extra challenge, use the following frame: "I was born on [day], therefore my name is [name]."

6

Directions – *Àkwàǹkyèrέ*

6.1   Pointers to note – *ǹhwὲsòɔ́ bí*

Twi	*English*
nìfá	right
bὲǹkúḿ	left
nìfá só	right (hand) side
bὲǹkúḿ só	left (hand) side
ǹkyéémú / ὲhó	beside
m̀fíḿfíní	middle
èmú	inside
àkyíré	behind
àníḿ	in front of
àníḿ tὲὲ	straight ahead
àpùὲέ	east
àtɔ́éέ	west
àtífí	north
ànààfóɔ́	south
ὲrékɔ́ àtɔ́éέ	towards west

ɛ̀rékɔ́ àpùèɛ́	towards east
ɛ̀kwáń	road / path / way
ǹkwàǹtá	junction
ǹtwàhó	roundabout
àséɛ́	under
ɛ̀sóró / ɛ̀só	up / top / in the sky
dùá nó ásé	under the tree
bépɔ́ nó só / àpàm̀pàm̀	on top of the mountain
bépɔ́ nó hó	beside the mountain

6.2 Some directional expressions – *Ǹsɛ́m̀ bí à ɛ̀fá àkwàǹkyɛ̀rɛ́ hó*

Twi	English
Kɔ̀ w'àním̀ tèè.	Go straightforward.
Kɔ̀ àkyíré.	Go back.
Kɔ̀ nìfá só.	Go to the right (hand side).
Kɔ̀ bèǹkúm̀ só.	Go to the left (hand side).
Mà
nè nìfá só.	Turn towards right (hand side).
Mànè bèǹkúm̀ só.	Turn towards left (hand side).
Br̀à àkyíré.	Come back.
Gyìnà hɔ́.	Stand/stop there.
Tènà m'àkyí	Sit behind me.
Hwɛ̀ sóró / fám̀.	Look upwards / downwards.
Hwɛ̀ wò nífá só.	Look at your right (hand) side.
Kɔ̀ w'àním̀ ná mánè nìfá só.	Go straight and turn to the right.
Ɛ̀fírí àtífí kósí ànàafɔ́ɔ́.	From the north to the south.
Àwìá púé wɔ̀ àpùéɛ́ ná àtɔ̀ wɔ̀ àtɔ̀éɛ́.	The sun rises in the east and sets in the west.
Ɛ̀dáń á ɛ̀tɔ́ só náń wɔ̀ bèǹkúm̀ só nó mú nà mètéɛ́.	It is the 4th house from the left that I live in.
Sàfòà nó dà ɛ̀pónó nó <u>só</u> / <u>àsé</u>.	The key is <u>on</u> / <u>under</u> the table.
Àbòfrá nó hyɛ̀ né mààmé ákyí.	The child is behind (tied to the back of) his/her mother.
Pàpá nó tè dáń nó áním̀.	The man is sitting in front of the house.
Mètè ɛ̀pónó / pɔ̀ǹkɔ́ nó só.	I'm sitting on the <u>table</u> / <u>horse</u>.
Kúsíé hyɛ́/ dá àmènà nó mú.	A rat is inside the hole.

6.3 A dialogue about directions – *Ǹkɔmmɔdíe bí à ɛ̀fá àkwàǹkyèrɛ́ hó*

	Twi		English
Kyèí:	Dèdé, kɔ̀ àsásó hɔ́ nà fá ɛ̀tòá nó áà ɛ̀sí ɛ̀pónó nó áse̩ nó bfɛ̀ mè.	**Kyei:**	Dede, go into the living room and bring the bottle under the table to me.
Dèdé:	Yòò! Éí, èmú yɛ̀ dùrù pápá. Ɛ̀déɛ́n nà ɛ̀wɔ́ mú?	**Dede:**	All right! Ai, it is very heavy. What is inside (the bottle)?
Kyèí:	Ɛ̀yɛ̀ àdúró. Fá kɔ́ Kégyétíá kɔ́má wó mààmé.	**Kyei:**	It is medicine. Take it to Kejetia and give it to your mother.
Dèdé:	Ɛ̀hé nà Kégyétíá wɔ́? Mɛ́fá kwáń bɛ̀ń só ákɔ́ hɔ́?	**Dede:**	Where is Kejetia? How do I get there (which road will lead me there)?
Kyèí:	Kɔ̀ w'àníḿ tèè kɔ̀sí sɛ̀ wóbɛ́húnú sòtɔ́ɔ̀ bí áà yɛ́átwérɛ́ àníḿ sɛ́ 'Ònyàmé túmí'. Wódúrù hɔ́ áà, màne̩ fá bènkúḿ só.	**Kyei:**	Go straightforward until you see a store with the inscription: 'God's power'. At this point, turn towards your left.
Dèdé:	Yòò! Mèmàne̩ fá bènkúḿ só áà, mény̩ɛ́ dɛ́ń bíó?	**Dede:**	All right! After turning towards my left, what should I do next?
Kyèí:	Kɔ̀ w'àníḿ tèè kɔ̀sí sɛ̀ wóbɛ́hú ǹkwàǹtá bí. Ɛ̀hɔ́ nó, wódàne̩ w'àní hwɛ́ wò nìfá só áà, Kégyétíá árá né nó.	**Kyei:**	Go straight until you see a junction. At this point, if you look towards your right, you will see Kejetia.
Dèdé:	Kégyétíá kɛ́sɛ́é yí né mú ǹnípá pìì yí, méy̩ɛ́ dɛ́ń áhù mé mààmé ápátá?	**Dede:**	How do I find my mother's shed /store with Kejetia being that big and with a lot of people?
Kyèí:	Nyà ǹtòbòàsɛ̀é. Wómá w'àní só hwɛ́ sóró kàkŕá áà, wóbɛ́húnú ɛ̀dáń téńténé bí. Sàà ɛ̀dáń yí áse̩ pɛ̀ɛ̀ nà wó mààmé sótɔ́ɔ̀ wɔ́.	**Kyei:**	Be patient. If you look a little up, you'll see a tall building. It is on the ground floor of this building that your mother's store is.
Dèdé:	Ɔ̀nó ǹkó árá sótɔ́ɔ̀ nà ɛ̀wɔ́ hɔ́?	**Dede:**	Is her store the only one there?
Kyèí:	Dàábí! Wódúrù áà, sòtɔ́ɔ̀ áà ɛ̀tɔ́ só núḿ fírí wò nífá só nó mú nà wóbɛ́hú wó mààmé.	**Kyei:**	No! If you reach there, you will find your mother in the fifth store from your right.
Dèdé:	Yòò! Mèrèkɔ́ àbà sèèséí árá.	**Dede:**	All right! I'll be back soon.
Kyèí:	Mèdàààsè! Ǹní ágórɔ́ wɔ̀ kwáń mú óò!	**Kyei:**	Thank you! Don't play on the way!

Exercises

1. In Akan-Twi, give someone directions from your dormitory/residence to the classroom, and the back again from the classroom to your residence.

2. Stand next to you tutor, teacher, or classmate and then give him/her directions using the vocabulary and phrases presented in this chapter (turn to your left, look upwards, etc.). Then, trade with him/her and follow similar instructions from your tutor/classmate.

3. With your knowledge on how locations are identified in Akan-Twi, describe the following pictures in Akan-Twi, e.g.:

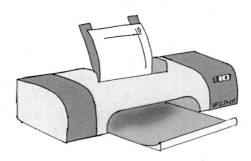

Kŕátàá nó hyὲ àfìdíé nó mú.
'The paper is in the machine.'

(a)

Kàá nó rè _____.
'The car is taking a right turn'.

(b)

i. Pàpá nò _____ pɔ̀ǹkɔ́ nó _____.
   'The man is sitting on the horse'

ii. Pɔ̀ǹkɔ́ nó rè _____ _____.
   'The horse is going forward'.

(c)

i. Ǹkwàdàá nó _____ m̀fòyíní nó _____.
   'The children are sitting in front of the picture.'

ii. M̀fòyíní nó _____ ǹkwàdàá nó _____.
   'The picture is hanging behind the children.'

iii. Bɔ́ɔ̀lò nó _____ àkwàdàá nó náń _____.
   'The ball is lying beside the child.'

(d)

    i. Ǹnípá nó tètè kyìnìèέ nó _____.
       'The people are sitting under the umbrella.'

    ii. Ɔbáá nó _____ɔbàrímá nó _____ só.
        'The woman is sitting at the left of the man.'

4. Referring to this map of Ghana, describe the orientation of one region to the other. For example, where is the Volta Region with respect to the Eastern Region? Where is the Ashanti (a.k.a. Asante) Region with respect to the Brong Ahafo Region?

5. Wherever you are, find a city map. Ask and give directions to your classmates between key points on the map such as the school(s), market(s), etc.

7

Family Relations – *Àbùsùàbɔ́*

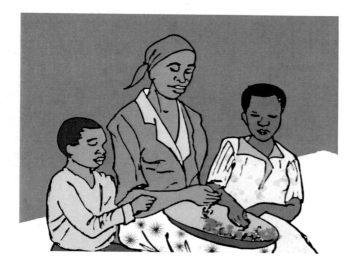

Traditionally, the people of Akan cultures practice the extended family system. The adoption of certain Western practices and ways of living continues to undermine the practice of the extended family system. In the big cities, the nuclear family system is now becoming common. This is due to the present economic conditions and the desire of parents to have fewer children. However, the extended family continues to play certain traditional roles. In the villages, the extended family system is predominantly practised. This may be due to the maintenance of certain practices, *e.g.* polygamy, matrilineal inheritance, etc., and the desire to keep particular lineages together.

Most Akan-speaking cultures trace their lineage through their mothers, so we say that the Asante, Fante, and Akuapem are a matrilineal societies. One significant characteristic of a matrilineal society is that a son does not inherit from his father, but rather his uncle (*i.e.* his mother's brother). It is believed that a nephew shares the same blood lineage with his uncle(s) through his mother (the uncle's sister by blood).

7.1   Family Composition – *àbùsùà ǹnìpá bí*

Twi	English
pàpá ; páàpá	Mister / man / father; father
mààmé / énó	mother
nàná	old person or grandparent / title of a king
wɔfà	uncle
sèwáá	aunt
ònùá	sibling
ònùá bárímá	brother
ònùá báá	sister
ònùá pányín	elder sibling
ònùá kúmáá	younger sibling
wɔfààsé	nephew
wɔfààsé wáá	niece
mààmé / pàpá núá bá	cousin (mother's / father's sibling's child)
àséẃ	father- / mother- / daughter- / son-in-law
àkòǹtá	brother-in-law (between male and male)
àkùmàá	sister-in-law (between female and female)
òkúnú	husband
ɔyéré	wife
m̀péná	boyfriend / girlfriend
àbákáṅ	first born
àdàǹtɛ́m̀	middle (somewhere in-between)
káàkyíré	last born
màánú	second born
máṅsá né mèǹsá	third born
àtá	male twin
àtàá	female twin
táwíá	a person who is born after twins

7.2   Terms of Identity – *àhyèǹsòdéɛ́ ńyínàsòɔ́ bí*

Twi	English
ɔbáá	female
ɔbàrímá	male
àbábáàwá / àkètèésíá / àwùràbá	lady

àbřántéɛ́ / àbřàntéwá	gentleman (young man)
òwúrà	Mister / Lord
òwúràyéré	Missus
àbááyéwá	girl
àbɛ̀ɛ̀múwá / àbɛ̀ɛ̀máá	boy
àbèrèwá	old woman
àkɔ̀kòrá / àkòrá	old man
àbèrèwà / àkɔ̀kòrà pósópósó	very old woman / man
tɔ̀tɔ̀fèéwá	infant / baby
àbɔ̀fŕá / àkwàdàá	child
pànyíń	elder / adult
téńtéń	tall
tìétíá	short
téátéá / hwéáhwéá	thin / slim
kɛ̀séɛ́	big / fat
bósíé	well-built
kɔ̀sórókɔ́bɔ́	shapeless
	(big upper on small lower)
kórókóŕówá	cute
tùǹtùm̀	dark (in complexion)
kɔ̀kɔ́ɔ́	fair (in complexion)
òbřòníí	white person
àhòɔ̀fɛ́	beauty / handsome
múmɔ́	ugly person

7.3 Some expressions about identity – *Ǹkèkàé bí á ɛ̀fá àhyɛ̀ǹsòdéɛ́ ńyínàsòɔ́ hó*

Twi	English
Mèyɛ̀ káàkyíré.	I am a last-born.
Kòfí yɛ̀ m'àbákáń.	Kofi is my first child.
Mé núá yèí yɛ́ táwíá.	This brother of mine comes after twins.
Ǹtààfóɔ́ hó yɛ̀ àníká.	Twins are interesting.
Mé pàpá yɛ̀ tìétíá kɔ̀kɔ́ɔ́.	My father is short and fair in complexion.
Mèyɛ̀ téńtéń sénè wó mààmé kúnú nó.	I'm taller than your mother's husband.
Kòfí wɔfà mààmé yɛ̀ mé ńsó mé nànáà.	Kofi's uncle's mother is also my grandmother.
Mé mààmé/pàpá núá bá nó áwáré wò wɔ̀fàdàséwá kórókóŕówá nó.	My cousin has married your cute niece.
Àbábáàwá nó bósí (tà).	The lady is (completely) well-built.

Àbááyéwá bíárá yὲ mé núá báá ὲnà àbὲὲmáá bíárá ńsó yέ mé núá bárímá.	Every girl is my sister and every boy is my brother.

7.4 A dialogue about family relations – Ǹkͻmmͻ́díe bí à ὲfá nìpàsú né àbùsùàbͻ́ hó

	Twi		English
Sὲbé:	Kùsí, wó màámé né hwáń (hwáń né wó màámé)?	**Sebe**	Kusi, who is your mother?
Kùsí:	Mé màámé né Yàá Dèdé.	**Kusi:**	My mother is Yaa Dede.
Sὲbé:	Ǹtì sὲ mèhyìá wó màámé áà, mέ yέ dέń áhù nó?	**Sebe**	So, if I meet your mother, how will I know it is her?
Kùsí:	Ͻyὲ tùntùḿ, téńtéń, kὲséέ.	**Kusi:**	She is dark in complexion, tall and plump.
	Àféí ńsó, ͻwͻ tírénwíí pìì.		Also, she has a lot of hair.
Sὲbé:	Wóbétúmí ákà àhyὲǹsòdéé áfófóró bí ákà hó?	**Sebe**	Can you say/give further descriptive markers?
Kùsí:	Àáné! N'àní ḿmá sòsò.	**Kusi:**	Yes! Her eyes are big.
	Áféí ńsó, nè hwéné yὲ téátéá fὲféέfέ.		Also, her nose is long and beautiful.
Sὲbé:	Yòò! Wówͻ ànùànóḿ séń?	**Sebe**	All right! How many siblings do you have?
Kùsí:	Ṁmὲὲnsá; ḿmáá ḿmìènú nà bàrímá bààkó.	**Kusi:**	Three; two girls and one boy.
	Mé nà mὲtͻ só náń.		I am the fourth.
Sὲbé:	Éńtí wó né káàkyíré.	**Sebe**	So, you are the last-born.
	Wó núánóḿ nó mú bì áwáré?		Are any of your siblings married?
Kùsí:	Àáné! Ṁmáá nó mú pànyíń nó áwáré áwͻ ḿmàrímá ḿmìènú.	**Kusi:**	Yes! The eldest of the females is married and has two boys.
Sὲbé:	Ὲyέ, ńtí wówͻ wͻfààsénóḿ ḿmìènú.	**Sebe**	Good, so you have two nephews.
	Wͻfààséwááńóḿ ńsóéέ?		What about nieces?
Kùsí:	Mé núá bárímá nó né nè ḿpéná ńsó áwͻ ḿmáá ńtààfóͻ.	**Kusi:**	My brother (the eldest) has female twins with his girlfriend.
	Éńtí mèwͻ wͻfààséwááńóḿ ńsó.		So, I also have three nieces.
Sὲbé:	Óò! Éńtí wó núá nó ńwáréὲ ǹtààfóͻ nó màámé nó. Ádέń?	**Sebe**	Oh! So your brother hasn't married the twins' mother. Why?
Kùsí:	Mèǹníḿ déέ, nàńsó mègyé dí sὲ mé sèwáá né mé nànà ḿpέ ͻbáá nó ásέḿ ńtírá.	**Kusi:**	I don't know, but I believe it is because my aunt and my grandparent don't like the lady.
Sὲbé:	Ádέń? Ͻbáá né hó ńyέ fὲ ànáá.	**Sebe**	Why? Isn't the lady beautiful?
Kùsí:	Dàbí! Nè hó yέ fὲ páá, ńsó wͻtàá ká sὲ ͻḿmú ádéέ.	**Kusi:**	No! She is very beautiful, but they always say that she is disrespectful.

Sὲbɛ́:	Éì! Y'àbùsùàfóɔ́ yí!	Sebe	Ai! These relatives of ours!
	Yòò! Mὲrèkɔ́ m'àkóńtá hɔ́, àntì àkyíré yí.		All right! I am going to my brother-in-law's, so see you later.
Kùsí:	Yòò, bàábàí. Ὲyɛ́ áà kyèà nó má mὲ.	Kusi:	All right, bye-bye. Send my regards to him.

The Family Tree – *àbùsùàbɔ́ dúá*

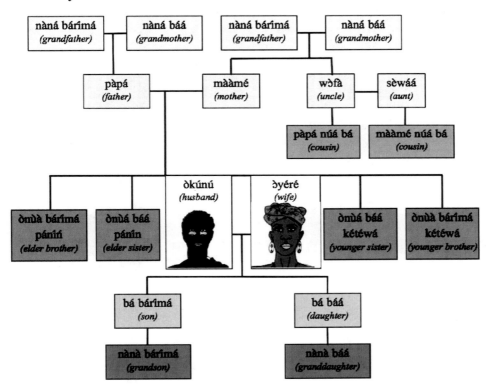

Exercises

1. Answer the following questions in Twi:

	Question	Answer
e.g.,	*Hwáń né wó pàpá?*	Mé pàpá né Òwúrà Kòfóɔ́.
a.	Wó màamé yɛ̀ tùǹtùm̀ ànáá kɔ̀kɔ́ɔ?	_____
b.	Wó núánóm̀ m̀máá yɛ́ sɛ́ń?	_____
c.	Wó màamé yɛ̀ mé núá, ǹtì mèyɛ̀ wò déɛ́ń?	_____

2. Looking at your physical features and those of a friend or a classmate sitting beside you, tell the rest of the class about the physical differences between yourself and him or her.

   e.g., *Ɔ̀yɛ̀ tùǹtùm̀ sénè mè.*

   'He/she is darker in complexion than me.'

3. Tell your classmates the ages of all your siblings, cousins, children and/or parents, in Akan-Twi.

4. Discuss—in Twi if you can, otherwise in English—roughly how old you would consider a person to be for you to use the following terms: *nàná, òwúrà, àbèrèwá, pànyíń,* and *nùá.* Are some 'safer' to use than others in instances where you can't tell a person's age for sure?

5. Without looking into your book, try to answer the questions in the following kinship
   diagram in Twi:

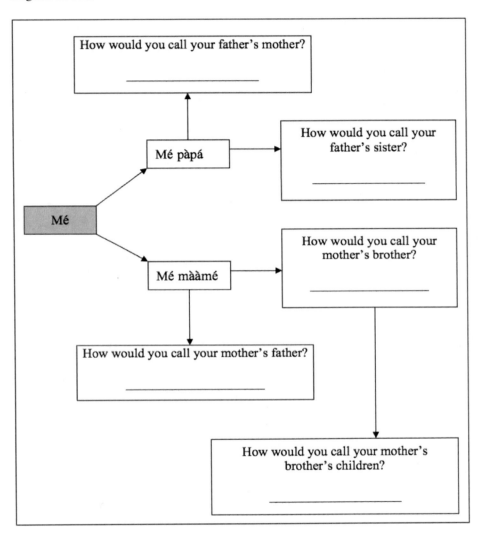

8

Types of Food: Meat, Vegetables & Fruits –
Ǹnùàné: ɛ̀náḿ, Àtòsòdéɛ̀ né Ǹnùàbá Áhóróɔ́ Bí

The Akan people have a variety of traditional foods made out of various starches, meat, vegetables, and fruits. In this chapter, we identify some of the most common of these, to prepare you for Ghana's many culinary delights.

8.1   Some types of food – *ǹnùàné áhódóɔ́ bí*

Twi	English
àbéńkwáń	palm-nut soup
àbètéɛ̀	dried, milled and cooked meal of cassava
àbòmúú	stew / gravy
àbùnàbúnú	cocoyam leaves soup
àbùró	maize / corn
àdùá	beans
àkákádúró	ginger
àm̀pèsíé	cooked cassava/plantain/cocoyam/yam
àǹwá	oil

àǹwámóó	fried rice (*i.e.*, cooked oiled-rice)
àsíkyíré	sugar
àyúó	millet
bàǹkú	milled, fermented and cooked meal of maize
bàǹkyè	cassava
bàyéré	yam
bɔɔ̀déɛ́	plantain
dìéhúó	dried, milled and cooked meal of maize
dɔ̀kónó	milled, fermented, and cooked meal of maize, wrapped in leaves
èsám̀	flour
ɛ̀mó	rice / steamed rice
ɛ̀móótúó	rice balls
ɛ̀tɔ́	mashed cassava/plantain/cocoyam/yam
ɛ̀wóɔ́	honey
fúfúó	pounded cassava/plantain/cocoyam/yam
gàaré / gàalé	gaari (a cereal made from cassava)
kókó	porridge
kòkòǹté	cassava flour or dried cassava
kòsùá	eggs
màǹkàní	cocoyam
m̀pìhòó	semi-milled maize porridge
ǹgó / ǹgwó	red oil (*i.e.*, oil from palm-nut)
ǹkàtèɛ́	groundnut
ǹkàtèǹkwáń	groundnut soup
ǹkàtèǹkòǹtó	mixed soup of groundnut & cocoyam leaves
ǹkwáń	soup
ǹkyéné	salt
ǹkyɛ́kyérá	corn, steamed in leaves
nófósúó	(breast) milk
nùhùú	cooked and liquefied cocoyam in palm nut oil
páánòó	bread

8.2 Fish and meat – *àdwéné né nám̀*

Twi		English	
Àdwéné:		**Fish:**	
	ámàné		dried fish
	mɔ̀mɔ̀né		salted fish (soft)
	kòóbì		salted fish (dried)
	àpàtéré		smoked herring(s)
	kɔ́tɔ́		crab
	mɔ́ǹkɔ́		shrimp(s)

Ènáḿ:		Meat:
	nàǹtwìnáḿ	beef
	òdwáánáḿ	mutton
	prὲkònáḿ	pork
	dwànáḿ	bush-meat / game-meat
	àkókónáḿ	chicken
	dábòdábònáḿ	duck
	àkòǹfὲḿnáḿ	guinea-fowl
	křókřókòkò	turkey
	kyèkyèngá	kebab

8.3   Some vegetables – àtòsòdéέ bí

Twi	English
gyèéné	onion
mὲkó	pepper
nyààdóá	garden-egg (eggplant / aubergine)
ǹtóòsè	tomatoes
ǹkòǹtómmìré	cocoyam leaves
m̀mìré	mushroom
ǹkrùmá	okro / okra
ǹkátéέ	groundnut / peanut

8.4   Some fruits – ǹnùàbá bí

Twi	English
àǹkáà	orange
tàǹgàréè	tangerine
àmáńgò	mango
áprò	apple
bèsé	cola-nut
páyà	pea (US English = avocado)
bòòfré	pawpaw (US English = papaya)
kùbé	coconut
kòòkóò	cocoa
àbé	palm-nut
àbròbέ	pineapple
kwàdú	banana

8.5 Some expressions about food, vegetables and fruits – *Ǹsέḿ bí á ὲfá àdùàné, ǹtòsòdéέ né ǹnùàbá bí*

Twi	English
tù bàǹkyὲ, *etc.*	to harvest (uproot) cassava, etc.
kyὲ gyèéné né ǹtóòsè, *etc.*	to fry onions and tomatoes, etc.
nòà ὲmóó, àdùàné nó, *etc.*	to cook rice / the food, etc.
yὲ ǹkwáń, àdùàné, *etc.*	to cook soup, food, etc.
dì àdùàné nó, *etc.*	to eat the food, etc.
nòḿ ǹsúó, ǹkwáń, *etc.*	to drink water, soup, etc.
wè náḿ, bèsé, *etc.*	to chew meat, cola-nut, etc.
tè áprò, ǹkrùmá, mὲkó, *etc.*	to pluck apples, okro, pepper, etc.
twà bòòdéέ, kwàdú, àbùró, *etc.*	to harvest (cut) plantain, banana, corn, etc.
dwà bòòdéέ, bàǹkyὲ, *etc.*	to peel the skin of plantain, cassava, etc. with knife
hwànè kwàdú, *etc.*	to peel the skin of banana, etc. by hand
nù àbέ nó	to harvest (cut out from the palm-tree) the palm-nut
nù ǹkwáń, kókó, *etc.* mú	to stir soup, porridge, etc.
kyὲ ànkáà	to share oranges / to donate oranges
yàḿ mὲkó, ǹyààdóá, *etc.*	to grind pepper, garden-eggs, etc.
hònò ǹkyéné, àsíkyíré, *etc.*	to dissolve salt, sugar, etc.

8.6 Some cooking utensils and equipment – *àdùànènóá hó ǹnéέmá bí*

Twi	English
kyὲǹsèé	silver (for cooking)
kúkúó	pot (made out of clay)
àhèná	cooler (earthenware used to store drinking water)
dàdèséń / dààséń	aluminium cooking ware
àpáḿpáń	big flat cooking ware
àtèré	spoon
ǹkwàǹtèré	ladle (serving spoon)
kúwá	cup
prétè	plate
sònèé	sieve
bòkyéá	tree-stoned stove/cooker
kròpóòtò	coal pot
ègyá	fire
wàdúró	mortar
wómá	pestle

àpòtòyówá	grinder (a pot within which things are ground)
ètá / tàpòré	grinder (a carved wooden object to grind things in)
sékáń	knife
pàpà	fan (used to increase the fire)

8.7 A dialogue about types of food, vegetables and fruits – *Ǹkɔmmɔ́díe bí à ɛ̀fá ǹnùàné, ǹtòsòdéɛ́ né ǹnùàbá bí hó*

	Twi		English
Yáà:	Kùsí, àdùàné bɛ́ń páá nà wópɛ́?	**Yaa:**	Kusi, what food do you like best / what is your favourite food?
Kùsí:	Àdùàné áà mèpɛ́ páá né bàǹkú né ǹkàtèǹkwáń áà ǹkrùmá kàkŕá gú só. Nà wóɛ́?	**Kusi:**	The food I like best / my favourite food is banku with groundnut soup with a little okro on it. What about you?
Yáà:	Mé ńsó mépɛ̀ ɛ̀mó né àbòmúú. Ńsó mètàá dí gàà ré àdùá.	**Yaa:**	I also like rice with stew. But I normally eat gari and beans.
Kùsí:	Ádɛ́ń ńtí(á)?	**Kusi:**	Why?
Yáà:	Èfìrísɛ́ ɛ̀mó né àbòmúú bóɔ́ yɛ̀ dèn dódó.	**Yaa:**	Because rice with stew is too expensive.
	Àféí ńsó, gààré né àdùá mú yɛ̀ dù sénè ɛ̀mó né àbòmúú.		Also, gari with beans is heavier (i.e., the meal keeps one going for a long time) than rice and stew.
Kùsí:	Ɛ̀yɛ̀ nòkóré.	**Kusi:**	It is true.
	Wónóm̀ ǹsúó gú só dèɛ̀ áà, wóbɛ́méé dà mú nó nyìnáá.		If you drink water to supplement it, then, it can take you throughout the whole day.
Yáà:	Ɛ̀nó árá nà wóáká nó.	**Yaa:**	You have said it all.
Kùsí:	Nà ǹnùàbá ńsóɛ́? Ɛ̀mú dèɛ̀ ɛ̀wɔ́ hé nà wótáá díé?	**Kusi:**	What about fruits? Which one of them do you usually eat?
	Mé dèɛ̀ mèpɛ̀ kwàdú páá.		I like bananas very much.
Yáà:	Mé ńsó sàá árá, ńsó ɛ̀yɛ́ áà mèdè ǹkátéɛ́ áà yɛ́átótó bɔ́ só.	**Yaa:**	Me too, but I eat them with roasted groundnuts.
	Sàá mà nó yédɛ̀ páá.		They are very delicious that way.
Kùsí:	Sáà? Ɛ́nnèɛ̀ mɛ́sɔ́ áhwɛ́.	**Kusi:**	Really? Then, I will try.
	Mèrèkɔ̀ tétè àǹkàá ámà mé pàpá, ǹtì bàábàì.		I am going to pluck oranges for my father, so goodbye.
Yáà:	Sáà? Sɛ̀ wópɛ̀ áà, métúmí ábɛ̀bòá wó.	**Yaa:**	Is that so? If you like, I can come and help you.
Kùsí:	Yèí dèɛ̀ àsɛ̀m̀pá. Ɛ́nnèɛ̀ yɛ̀ńkɔ́.	**Kusi:**	This is good news. Then, let us go.
	Wóbɛ́túmí ábòá mé ámà mátù bàǹkyé ńsó kàkŕá?		Can you help me to harvest some cassava too?

Yáà:	Àáné, nàńsó mɛ́fá bànkyé kàkŕá ákɔ̀ mè fíé.	**Yaa:**	Yes, but Ill take a little of the cassava to my house.
Kùsí:	Óò, ɛ̀ǹyɛ́ hwèè. Mèdàasé píí.	**Kusi:**	Oh, it is all right (it is nothing). Thank you very much.
Yáà:	Bòà mè nà mé ḿmóá wò dèè sɛ́ àsɛ̀dá bíárá ńní mú o! Ṁpó mé nà ɛ̀sɛ́ sɛ́ mèdá wò àsé.	**Yaa:**	Helping each other demands no thanks. If there is, I should be thanking you.
Kùsí:	Ɛ̀yɛ̀ nòkórɛ́.	**Kusi:**	That is true.

Exercises

1. Looking at the list of food given in this chapter, can you write down the names of some others you have noted in your ethnic group, country, or surroundings that have not been mentioned?

2. Tell your friends about the food you like best and give reasons why you like those foods.

3. Identify and say aloud the Akan/Twi names of each of the types of food and cooking utensils in the following picture table.

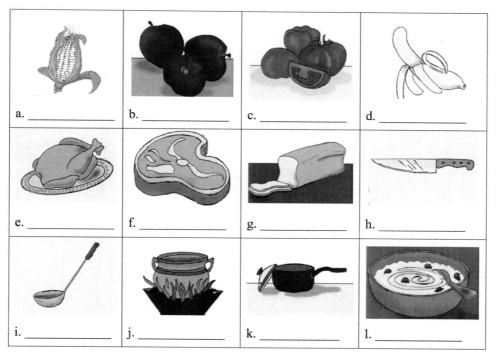

a. _____ b. _____ c. _____ d. _____

e. _____ f. _____ g. _____ h. _____

i. _____ j. _____ k. _____ l. _____

4. Use the names of some of the things in the above pictures to make up five sentences. For example, pretend you are ordering at a chop bar, or pretend you are teaching your younger sibling how to cook.

9

At the Market – *Wɔ Dwám / Ɛ̀dwá só*

Among Akan-speaking peoples, it is common to find an open-air market, rather than an enclosed store or supermarket, where retailers bring their goods to sell and consumers come to buy them. Indeed this kind of business setting is not unique to Ghana, but is a setting that can be found in many African countries and many other parts of the world.

In the case of the African setting, in particular, in the course of trading, there occurs a real bargaining on items being sold. In other words, unlike in the Western world, for instance, goods are not strictly pre-priced. Even where price tags are found on goods, one can still negotiate for a better deal, and in many cases the buyer is expected to do so. The following are some of the common expressions that one may hear at the market place and in the course of bargaining.

9.1 Some terms about buying and selling – *Ǹsɛ́ḿfùá bí à ɛ̀fá dwádíé hó*

Twi	English
àbòɔdéń	expensive
àdèfòdéɛ́	something cheap
àkyìngyé	argument / disagreement
ànódíé / ǹnìànòó	bargaining
àsìsíé	cheating
ɛ̀bóɔ́	price
ɛ̀ká	loss
fò	cheap
gyé	to take
ká bó mú	to put together
káń	to count
ká / sɔ́ hwɛ́	to try / test
kyèkyèrè	to wrap
má	to give
m̀fàsóɔ́	profit
ǹsésá	change
ǹtèsòɔ́	reduction
ǹtòsòɔ́	increment
'Sɛ́ń(sɛ́ń)?'	'How much?'
sìsì / bú	to cheat
sùsù	to measure/weigh
tè só	to reduce
tò só	to add to
tɔ́	to buy
tɔ́ń	to sell
tùà	to pay
twá	to cut

9.2 Things to note at the market – *Ǹnéɛ́má bí à yxE hú nò dwám̀*

Besides all the different foods one may find at the market, the following are just some of the hallmarks of a typical African marketplace.

Twi	English
àdèsr̀ɛ́fóɔ́	beggars
àfrɛ̀frɛ́	calls (from sellers)
àkáyáfóɔ́	carriers / helpers
àpónó	tables / stalls
àtɛ̀ǹníé	insults
àtòtòbótóḿfóɔ́	pickpockets

àtɔǹfóɔ́	sellers
àtɔfóɔ́	buyers
dàwùbɔ́fóɔ́	announcers
dédé	noise
ǹkònwá	chairs / stools
ǹkɔm̀mɔ́	conversations
ǹnóɔ́má pìì	many things
ǹnípá pìì	many people
ǹtèàmúú	shouting
ǹtɔkwá	quarrelling

9.3 Some useful expressions at the market – *Ǹsɛ̀m̀èká bí à ɛ̀hóɔ́ híá wxC dwám̀*

Twi	English
Mèpààkyɛ́ẃ	I beg you / please.
Tè mè só.	Reduce (the price) for me.
Tò mè só.	Increase (the amount of product) for me.
Màbɔ́ ká.	I've made a loss.
Mànyá m̀fàsóɔ́.	I've made a profit.
Yèí / Wèí bóɔ́ yɛ̀ sɛ́ń?	How much is this one?
Yèínóḿ / Wèínóḿ bóɔ́ sɛ́ń?	How much are these ones?
Yèí / Wèí bóɔ́ yɛ̀ sídì ɔhà.	This one costs a hundred cedis.
Né bóɔ́ yɛ̀ dèǹ.	It is expensive.
Mà mè ǹsésá.	Give me change.
Fà mè ǹsésá má mè.	Give me my change.
Kyèkyèrè má mè.	Wrap (it / them) for me.
Wóásísí mé.	You've cheated me.
(Ɛ̀yɛ́ áà) bɾ̀à bíó.	(Do) come again.

9.4 A dialogue in the market – *èdwám̀ ǹkɔm̀mɔ́díe bí*

	Twi		English
Tɔ́fóɔ́:	Mààmé, bòrɔ̀déé / kwàdú sá yí sɛ́ń?	**Buyer:**	Woman / Ma'am, how much is this bunch of plantain / banana?
Tɔ̀ǹfóɔ́:	Ɛ̀yɛ́ sídì àhàànù. Wópɛ̀ sɛ́ń? Sɛ̀ wótɔ́ bɾ̀ò èsá bààkó áà métè só ámà wò!	**Seller:**	It is two hundred cedis. How many do you want? If you buy more than one bunch, I'll reduce the cost for you!

Tɔ́fóɔ́:	Yòò! Ɛ́nèɛ̀ mèrètɔ́ àsá m̀mèɛ̀ǹsá. Né bóɔ́ béyɛ́ sɛ́ń?	**Buyer:**	All right! Then, I'll buy three bunches. How much will those cost?
Tɔ̀ǹfóɔ́:	Mɛ́té wò só sídì ɔ̀hà.	**Seller:**	I'll take away a hundred cedis.
	Ntì wóbɛ́túá sédì àhánúḿ.		Therefore, you'll pay five hundred.
	Màyɛ́ wò yíé.		I've given you a good deal.
Tɔ́fóɔ́:	Èì! Dàabí! Né bóɔ́ yɛ̀ déń. Mɛ́má wò sídí àhánáń, mèpàakyɛ́ẃ.	**Buyer:**	Ai! No! It is expensive. I will give you four hundred cedis, I plead with you.
Tɔ̀ǹfóɔ́:	Óò! Dàabí! Ɛ̀yɛ́ sàá áà ná wóásísí mé. Wó dèɛ̀ tùà sídì àhánáń né àdùònúḿ.	**Seller:**	Oh! No! With that I will be cheated. You take it for four hundred and fifty cedis.
Tɔ́fóɔ́:	Yòò! Mèdàasé.	**Buyer:**	All right! Thank you.
Tɔ̀ǹfóɔ́:	Nà wóǹtɔ́ hwèɛ̀ bíó?	**Seller:**	Won't you buy anything else?
Tɔ́fóɔ́:	*Hmm!* Mà mè màkó sídì àdùànáń ɛ́nà ànkàá ǹsó sídì àdùòsíá ǹká hó.	**Buyer:**	Hmm! Give me forty cedis worth of pepper and sixty cedis worth of oranges.
Tɔ̀ǹfóɔ́:	Yòò! Yɛ́í dèɛ̀ wóádì mè dwá ánɔ̀pá yí. Mèdàasé.	**Seller:**	All right! You have really helped me to increase my sales this morning. Thank you.
Tɔ́fóɔ́:	Kà nó nyìnáá bɔ́ mù ná ká mé ká kyérɛ̀ mè.	**Buyer:**	Add them up and tell me the total cost.
Tɔ̀ǹfóɔ́:	Ɛ̀ǹnɔ́ɔ̀sò. Wó kà nyìnáá yɛ́ sídì àhánúḿ né àdùònúḿ pɛ́. Méǹkyékyéré ḿmá wó ànáá?	**Seller:**	It is not much. You owe me only five hundred and fifty cedis. Should I wrap them for you?
Tɔ́fóɔ́:	Àáné! Mèdàasé.	**Buyer:**	Yes! Thank you.
Tɔ̀ǹfóɔ́:	Yɛ̀ǹní ásèdá. Wò ǹnéɛ́má níé. Ɛ́ǹnéɛ̀ bàábàé ó!!	**Seller:**	Not at all. Here are your goods. Goodbye!!
Tɔ́fóɔ́:	Bàí!	**Buyer:**	Bye!

Exercises

1. Name out loud some of the meat, vegetables, and fruit you may find at the market based on the vocabulary found in the previous chapter. What might your own personal shopping list include? Read your list aloud, in Akan-Twi.

2. Make up six expressions one can use at the market:

   e.g., *Mèrètɔ́ bàǹkyè.* = 'I'm buying cassava'

   (a) _____

   (b) _____

   (c) _____

   (d) _____

   (e) _____

   (f) _____

3. Act as a shopper at a market and buy something from a seller (as acted out by a friend or classmate). Be sure to purchase at least two different items, and be sure to practice bargaining!

4. Discuss—in Twi if you can, but if not, in English—how comfortable you are bargaining for prices. Do you have personal experience bargaining? What are some of the polite strategies you know of to bargain well? What are the best ones to get the lowest prices? Is there ever a time when you shouldn't bargain? When are you more likely to say *Tò mè só* than *Tè mè só*?

10

The Twi Colour Spectrum – *Twi Àhósú Áhódóɔ́*

The number of primary colours varies across different cultures and different languages. The colour spectrum in Akan-speaking cultures actually only has three primary colours: white, black and red. The other colours are secondary ones that are mostly identified with reference to an item that is typically of (or identified with) that colour.

10.1   Colours – *Àhósú*

Twi	English	
fítáá / fúfúó	white	
kɔkɔɔ́	red / fair-skinned	
tùntùm̀	black / dark-skinned	
wíémsú / bruu	blue	← 'the colour of the sky'
sàadéɛ́	yellow	← 'fats'
àhàbàamónó	green	← 'a new leaf'
sìkàkɔkɔ́ɔ́	gold	← 'the gold mineral'
nɛtèsú	brown	← 'soil'

10.2   Some basic expressions with colour – *Ǹkèkàé bí à ɛ̀fá àhósú hó*

Twi	English
àtàadéɛ́ kɔkɔɔ́ (àtàadé kɔ́kɔɔ́)	a red cloth (a red shirt)
Mèhyɛ̀ àtàdéɛ́ fítáá / fúfúó.	I am wearing a white shirt.
Àhósú áà m'ànı́ gyé hó páá né nɛtèsú.	My favourite colour is brown.
Mé pàpá yɛ̀ tùntùm̀.	My father is dark in complexion.
Mèyɛ̀ tùntùm̀ sénè mé pàpá.	I am darker than my father.
Mé pàpá pɛ̀ ǹnéɛ́má kɔkɔɔ́ páá.	My father likes things of red colour very much.
Kòmùàdéɛ́ nó yè sìkàkɔ́kɔ́ɔ́.	The necklace is (made of) gold.
Ǹsúó ńní áhósú.	Water doesn't have a colour / water is colourless.

49

Àwìá áhósú né sàdéɛ́.	The colour definition of the sun is yellow.
Àpòtòbíbré áhósú né àhàbààmónó.	The colour definition of spirogyra is green.

10.3 A dialogue about colour – Ǹkɔmmɔ́díe bí à ɛ̀fá àhósú áhódóɔ́ hó

	Twi		English
Àtá:	Yàá, m'àtáàdé (hyɛ́ɛ̀tè) yí tè sɛ́ń?	**Atta:**	Yaa, how is this shirt of mine?
Yàá:	Ɛ̀yɛ́ fɛ̀ (ɛ́ɛ̀fɛ̀) páá.	**Yaa:**	It is very nice.
	Nè túńtùm̀ nó ǹsó fàtá wò páá.		Its black colour also suits you very well.
	Mé pàpá wɔ̀ nè kɔ̀kɔ́ɔ́.		My father has a red one of it.
Àtá:	Mèdàse. Ná mèdwénè sɛ́ mèyɛ́ tùǹtùm̀ páá nó ńtí ɛ̀rém̀fàtà mé.	**Atta:**	Thank you. I thought it will not suit me because of my very dark complexion.
Yàá:	Nòkóré ní, mègyé dí sɛ́ àhàbààmónó áà àní dwó kàkrá béfátà wó ásèǹ tùǹtùm̀ yí.	**Yaa:**	Honestly, I believe that a light green one will suit you better than this black one.
Àtá:	Mè né wó yɛ́ àdwéné.	**Atta:**	I agree with you.
	Ná mèpɛ̀ sàdéɛ́ dèɛ́ ḿpó, ǹsó ná túńtùm̀ né wíémsú dèɛ́ pɛ́ nà ɛ̀wɔ́ hó.		I even wanted a yellow one, but only black and blue ones were there.
Yàá:	Ɛ̀yɛ́ ḿmòḿ, ɛ̀frìsɛ́ wóńyɛ́ túńtùm̀ pìì sɛ́ mé.	**Yaa:**	It is good though, because you're not very dark like me.
	Nà twòkòtò (trɔ́sà) àhyɛ́déɛ́ béń ná wódé bésí áséɛ́ (béhyɛ́)?		So, what colour of a pair of trousers will you use with it?
Àtá:	Mèwɔ̀ twòkòtò nètèsú mónó bí.	**Atta:**	I have a new brown pair of trousers.
	Wódwénè hó sɛ́ń?		What do you think about that?
Yàá:	Ɛ̀yɛ́ páá.	**Yaa:**	It is very good.
	Wóhyɛ́ m̀pàbòá túńtùm̀ ká hó dèɛ́ áà, ná ɛ̀nó árá né nó.		It will be great if you wear black shoes to go with it.
Àtá:	Mèǹní m̀pàbòà túńtùm̀.	**Atta:**	I don't have black shoes.
	Mèwɔ́ fìtáá fɛ̀ɛ̀fɛ́ bí ḿmòḿ áà ɛ̀bɛ́yɛ́.		I have a white pair though, which will be good.
Yàá:	Àà! Yɛ̀béfá nò sàà árá.	**Yaa:**	Ah! We will make do with it.
	Àdéɛ́ yí, dèɛ́ wówɔ́ árá né ńo.		After all, that is all that you have.

Exercises

1. Describe your own complexion in Twi as best you can. It may be helpful to contrast your complexion with those of your family members, friends, and/or classmates.

   e.g. *Mèyè kɔkɔɔ, ńsó* Jennifer *yè kɔkɔɔ sénè mè.*

   'I'm fair, but Jennifer is fairer than I.'

2. Mention the Twi names of the colours you see around you in class. You may also want to go outside of the classroom and name some more colours of things you see. In addition to practicing the colour names, use them in full sentences, such as those examples given in this chapter.

3. Describe the colours of your home to your classmates. What is the colour of your house? The door? The roof? The floor? The rugs? Try to give as much detail as possible.

4. With another classmate, pretend again that you are shopping at the market. This time, pretend that you are buying two types of fabric, contrasting in colour. Which colours will you buy? Don't forget to bargain!

5. Are there colour terms in your native language that you use frequently, but that aren't listed in this chapter? If you have an examples of those colours with you, ask your Akan instructor what colour term she/he would use to refer to that colour in Akan.

11

At School – *Sùkúù Mú*

In Ghana, a child normally starts formal education at the age of six. Before six, some children attend kindergarten (some children also attend nursery school). A child goes to primary school for a period of six years, *i.e.*, from class one ('primary one') to class six ('primary six').

After the primary school, a child enters the junior secondary school (JSS) for a period of three years, *i.e.*, from 'JSS one' to 'JSS three'. In the final year of the JSS education, students sit for entrance examination into the senior secondary school (SSS). Successful candidates go to SSS for three years, where they begin to specialize in a field of study.

In the final year of the SSS education, students take another examination to enter one of the higher institutions: universities, polytechnics, or teacher training colleges. One estimate in 2010 found that Ghana had 12,630 primary schools, 5,450 junior secondary schools, 503 senior secondary schools, 21 training colleges, 18 technical institutions, two diploma-awarding institutions and five public universities.

11.1 Things to note – *àhyɛ̀nsòdéɛ́ bí*

Twi	English
ɔkyèrɛ̀kyérɛ̀ní / tíkyàní	teacher / master / lecturer
ɔkyèrɛ̀kyérɛ̀ní bóáfóɔ́	teaching assistant
sùkúùní / sùání	student
kyèrɛ̀	to teach
twèrɛ̀	to write
twèrédúá	pen/pencil
twèrépónó	desk
twèrébéá	(black) board
twèrébéá átwérɛ̀déɛ́	chalk / marker
sùà (àdéɛ́)	to learn
àdèsùá	learning / education
ǹsɔ́hwɛ́	examination / test
ǹká hwɛ́	assignment
àsɛ̀m̀mìsá	question
ànóyíé / m̀mùàyɛ́	answer
sùàdáń (mú)	classroom
húnú	to know / to see
ɛ̀pónó	table
àkònwá	chair
m̀fíá / àbàá	cane
twá	to get (something) right
tí	to get (something) wrong
kásá	talk
dàdáń	dormitory
ǹnwómásó	library
gyìnàpéń	class / stage (of attendance)
àdìdíbéá	dining hall / canteen
ǹtɔ̀tɔ̀fèéwá súkúú	kindergarten / nursery
ǹhyɛ̀àséɛ́ súkúú	primary school
ǹtòàsóɔ́ súkúú	(junior/senior) secondary school
àkyèrɛ̀kyérɛ̀fóɔ́ ńtétèé súkúú	teacher training college/school
sùkúùpɔ̀ń	university

11.2   Some subjects/courses of study – *àdèsùàdéɛ́ bí*

Twi	English
àbákɔsɛ́m̀	history
àbóɔ́ né ǹnéɛ́má bí áà ɛ̀yɛ́ àsàasé hó	
ádèsùá	geology
àbɔ́déɛ́ mú ńhwèhwèɛ́	science
àbɔ́déɛ́ ásésúá	archaeology
àdùkyèrɛ́	pharmacy
àdúyɛ́	medicine
àdwéńsúsùà	psychology
àmámérɛ́ mú ádèsùá	cultural studies
àmáḿmúó mú ńhwèhwèɛ́	political science
àsàasé hó ńsɛ́m̀	geography
àséténá mú ádèsùá	social studies / sociology
Íngèlésè brɔ̀fó	English
dwádíé	business / commerce / training
m̀fìfìdéɛ́ né m̀móádómá hó ádèsùá	
/ ńhwèhwèɛ́	agricultural science
kásá hó ádèsùá	grammar / linguistics
m̀fìdìǹnwúmá hó ádèsùá	engineering
m̀mèrá / m̀mèràsúá	law (studies)
ǹkóńtá	mathematics
ǹsɛ̀m̀twèrɛ́ / dàwùbɔ́ hó ádèsùá	journalism
nwòm̀súá	music
nyàmè né nyàmèsɛ́m̀ mú ádèsùá	theology
nyàmèsɔ́m̀ mú ádèsùá	religious studies / theology
nyáńsá mú ńhwèhwèɛ́	philosophy
sìkàséséé	accounting
sìkàsɛ́m̀	economics
sìkàsíèsíé / sànàá	finance
sùàhúnú fófórɔ́	technology

11.3   Some statements relating to school – *Ǹsɛ́m̀ bí à ɛ̀fá sùkúù hó*

Twi	English
Wɔ̀yɛ̀ àkyèrɛ̀kyérɛfóɔ́.	They are teachers.
Àkyèrɛ̀kyèrɛfóɔ́ bìsá ńsɛ́m̀ pìì.	Teachers ask many questions.
Mèkyèrɛ́ ádéɛ́ wɔ̀ Ǹkràǹ.	I teach in Accra.
Tíkyàní nó ábɔ̀ / átwà mè àbàá.	The teacher has caned me.
Kòfí átwà nó nyìnáá.	Kofi has got all right.
Mètí náń.	I have got four wrong.

Ná ǹsɔ́kwɛ́ nó yɛ̀ dènè páá.	The examination was very difficult.
Ɔ̀yɛ̀ àbɔ́déɛ́ mú ádèsùà sùání.	He/she is a science student.
Yàẁ nìm̀ àdéɛ́ sénè wó.	Yaw is more intelligent than you.
Yáá sùá àsàasé hó ńsɛ́m̀.	Yaa studies geography / Yaa is a geography student.
Gáaná wɔ àsùkúàpɔ́ń núm̀.	Ghana has five universities.
Àsùkúùpɔ́ń m̀pɛ́ ádwúmáyɔ́.	Students don't like assignments.
Gáanáfóɔ́ pìì nìm̀ àkèǹkáń né àtwèrɛ́.	Many Ghanaians know how to read and write.
Òbíárá nìm̀ sɛ́ àbɔ́déɛ́ mú ńhwèhwèɛ́ yɛ̀ dèǹ páá.	Everyone knows that science is very difficult.
Twèrɛ́dúá mú yɛ̀ dúrú sénè sékáń.	The pen is mightier than the sword.
Àdèsùà hó hìá má àbɔ́fɛ́á bíárá.	Education is necessary for every child.

11.4   A dialogue about school – *Ǹkɔ̀mmɔ̀díe bí à ɛ̀fá sùkúù hó*

	Twi		English
Àfúá:	Àdò, wókɔ́ sùkúù wɔ hé?	**Afua:**	Ado, where do you attend school?
Àdó:	Mèkɔ́ Ɔ̀pókú Wàrè ǹtòàsòɔ́ sùkúù.	**Ado:**	I attend Opoku Ware secondary school.
Àfúá:	Ɛ̀wɔ́ héfá?	**Afua:**	Where is it located?
Àdó:	Ɛ̀wɔ́ Kùmásé Sàǹtáásé.	**Ado:**	It is located at Santasi in Kumasi.
Àfúá:	Nà wógyìnà sɛ́ń?	**Afua:**	So, in which class are you?
Àdó:	Mègyìnà gyìnápɛ́ń m̀mìènú.	**Ado:**	I am in form two.
	Nàǹsó, yèbùé sùkúù áà mɛ́kɔ̀ gyìnà pɛ́ń m̀mɛ̀ɛnsá.		But when school reopens, I will go to form three.
Àfúá:	Ɛ́nèɛ̀, wóbɛ́yɛ̀ pàníń.	**Afua:**	In that case, you will become a senior.
	Ńtí, móyɛ̀ɛ ǹsɔ́hwɛ́ àǹsáànà mórémá kwáń?		So, did you take examination before the vacation?
Àdó:	Àáné! Ná ǹkɛ́fátàá nó bí yɛ̀ dènè páá, nàǹsó mènìm̀ sɛ́ méfá mú.	**Ado:**	Yes! Some of the papers were very difficult, but I know I will pass.
Àfúá:	Àdèsùàdéɛ́ bɛ́ń nà wórésúá?	**Afua:**	What subject/course are you studying?
Àdó:	Mèrèsùá ǹhwèhwɛ́ mú áà ɛ̀fá àfìfìdéɛ́ né m̀móádómá hó.	**Ado:**	I am studying Agricultural science.
Àfúá:	Sàá! Ádɛ́ń ńtí nà wófáà àdèsùàdéɛ́ yèí?	**Afua:**	It that so! Why did you opt for this course?
Àdó:	Dàákyé, mèpɛ̀ sɛ́ mè né àkùàfóɔ́ yɛ́ àdwúmá.	**Ado:**	Someday / In the future, I want to work with farmers.
	Àdèsùàdéɛ́ yèí bɛ́bóá mé.		This course will help me.

	Nà wó ńsóέ?		What about you?
	Déέń nà wòrèsúá wɔ̀ sùkúùpɔ̀ń mú?		What are you studying at the university?
Àfúá:	Mèrèsùá m̀mèrá.	**Afua:**	I am studying law.
	M̀mòm̀, sὲ mèwìé áà mèpὲ sέ mèkyéré ádéέ.		But, when I complete, I want to teach.
Àdó:	Màté sὲ m̀mèràsúá yὲ dèǹ páá.	**Ado:**	I heard that law (studies) is very difficult.
	Ɛ̀yὲ nòkwáré?		Is that true?
Àfúá:		**Afua:**	No course is difficult or easy.
	Ɛ̀nó árá né sέ wóbέbɔ́ wò hó m̀mɔ́déń.		It is just a matter of working hard.
Àdó:	Ɛ̀yὲ nòkwáré.	**Ado:**	That is true.
	Nà ádéń ńtí nà wópέ sέ wókyéré ádéέ?		So why do you want to teach?
Àfúá:	ὲfìrìsέ m'àní gyὲ àdèkyὲrέ hó páá.	**Afua:**	Because I like teaching.
	Àféí ńsó, mègyé dí sὲ nìm̀dèέ nyìnáá áhyáséέ né àdèkyὲrέ.		Also, I believe that the root of all knowledge is teaching.

Exercises

1. Translate the following questions about school into Akan-Twi:

Question	Translation in Twi
a. In which class/stage is the boy?	_____
b. Kofi writes with pencil.	_____
c. I don't like teaching.	_____
d. Teachers cane children.	_____
e. Nobody likes examinations.	_____

2. Say the following Twi sentences about school out loud and translate them into English:

Question	Translation in Twi
a. Sùkúùfóɔ́ m̀pɛ́ ńsɔ́hwɛ́ yɛ́.	_____
b. Àbɔfrá nó átì nó nyìnáá.	_____
c. Òsɛ̀é yɛ̀ àdúyɛ́ sùání.	_____
d. M'àní gyè ǹkóńtá hó sénè Íngèlésè brɔ̀fó.	_____
e. Yàẁàwíé ǹtòàsóɔ́ súkúú.	_____

3. Tell your classmates what primary and secondary schools you went to, and ask them what school(s) they attended.

4. What were your favourite subjects when you were younger? What are they now? What were the most difficult subjects for you? If you're in a degree program now, what subject are you studying? Answer these questions in full sentences, in Twi, and ask these questions to your classmates.

5. Discuss—in Twi if you can, if not, then in English—how similar the educational structure is between Ghana and your home country. For example, do you know what 'form three' is? Do you know if the entrance requirements to Ghanaian universities are similar to those in your native country?

The Weather – *Èwíém Ńsèsàéɛ́*

In Ghana, as in many other countries in West Africa, there are only two main seasons. These are the dry and the rainy seasons. The weather becomes really hot (but barely humid) during the dry season, and is cooler in the rainy season. There is also a very short period of weather between the dry and cold seasons called *harmattan*.

12.1 The weather conditions – *èwíéḿ ǹsèsàéɛ́ ágóròɔ́ bí*

Twi	English
ǹsùó	water; rain
àsúkɔ́twèá	ice-rain
àwìá	sun
ɔ̀pɛ́	harmattan
	(a type of dusty wind)
ǹsùtɔ́bérɛ́	wet season; rainy season
	(May – October)
àwìbɔ́bérɛ́	dry season
	(November – April)
ɔ̀pɛ́bérɛ́	harmattan period
	(December – February)
àwɔ́	cold
àhúhúró	warmth
m̀fràmá	wind

12.2 Some expressions about the weather – *Ǹkèkàé bí à ɛ̀fá èwíéḿ ǹsèsàéɛ́ hó*

Twi	English
Àwɔ́ dè mè.	I feel cold.
Àhúhúró dè mè.	I feel hot / warm
Ɛ̀yɛ̀ ǹsùtɔ́bérɛ́ mú.	It is the rainy season.
Yɛ̀wɔ̀ ǹsùtɔ́bérɛ́ mú.	We are in the rainy season.
Yɛ̀wɔ̀ àwìbɔ́bérɛ́ mú.	We are in the dry season.
M̀fràmá rèbɔ́.	The wind is blowing. / It is windy.
Ǹsùó rètɔ́ áà, àgínàdàá dwìdwá.	When it rains, lighting occurs.
Ǹsùó rètɔ́ dènnéédéń.	It is raining heavily.
Ǹsùó ábò mè.	The rain has made me wet.
Ɔ̀pɛ́bérɛ́ mú, ǹsùó ǹńtɔ́.	During harmattan, it does not rain.
Ɔ̀pɛ́bérɛ́ mú, àwìá ǹtɔ́ ḿpó áà ná àwɔ́ wɔ̀ḿ.	During harmattan, even if the sun shines, it is still cold.
Ɔ̀pɛ́ áfà mé.	Harmattan has dried up my body.
Màhú nyàǹkòǹtɔ́ń.	I have seen a rainbow.
Sùkyèrɛ̀má ǹtɔ́ wɔ̀ Gáánà.	It does not snow in Ghana.

12.3 A dialogue about the weather – *Ǹkɔ̀mmɔ̀díe bí à ɛ̀fá wíém̀ ńsὲsàɛ̀ hó*

	Twi		English
Kùsí:	Ànwùméré yí, ǹsúó bɛ́tɔ́.	**Kusi:**	Tonight, it will certainly rain.
Nàná:	Ádɛ́ń ńtí nà wóréká sàá?	**Nana:**	Why are you saying that?
	Wóhùù déɛ́ń?		What did you see?
Kùsí:	Àwìá bɔ̀ɔ̀ ɛ̀nné páá.	**Kusi:**	The sun shone heavily today.
	Àféí ńsó àyɛ́ sɛ́dèɛ̀ ǹsúó ámúná nó.		Also, from the signs in the sky, it looks like it is going to rain.
Nàná:	Ébía, ǹànsó sɛ́dèɛ̀ m̀fràmá rèbɔ̀ yí dèɛ̀, mènnyé ǹní sé ɛ̀sɛ́tɔ́.	**Nana:**	Maybe, but from the way the winds are blowing, I don't believe it will rain.
Kùsí:	Ǹsùtɔ́bérɛ́ mú séî dèɛ̀, m̀fràmá bɔ́ m̀pó áà ɛ̀nyɛ́ hwèɛ̀.	**Kusi:**	In the rainy reason even the winds are nothing.
	Ámúná nó dèɛ̀ ɛ̀bɛ́tɔ́ páá.		Once the sky shows signs of rain, it will rain heavily.
Nàná:	Àà, yɛ̀rèhwɛ́ dèɛ̀ Nyàmé bɛ́yɛ́.	**Nana:**	Well, we will see what God will do.
	M̀mɔ̀m̀, ɛ̀tɔ́ ná sὲ àntɔ́ kɛ̀sé áà ɛ̀dè àhúhúró bɛ́bá.		However, if it doesn't rain heavily, the weather will become hot.
Kùsí:	Ɛ̀yɛ̀ nòkwáré. Ńsó yɛ̀bɛ́fá nò sàá árá.	**Kusi:**	It is true. But let us take it that way.
	Ǹsúó rètɔ́ yí dèɛ̀ ɛ́ǹkyɛ́ nà àwɔ́ ábà.		Now that it is raining it will not be long before the weather gets cold.
Nàná:	Mègyé dí sàá.	**Nana:**	I believe so.
	Yòò! Mèrèkɔ̀dá ǹtì ɔ̀kyéná. Dà yíé.		All right! I'm going to sleep, so see you tomorrow. Sleep well.
Kùsí:	Yòò! Nàná, mé ńsó mɛ́kɔ́ ákɔ̀dá sèèséí árá.	**Kusi:**	All right! Nana, I'll also go to bed very soon.
	Nyàmé m̀má àdèpá ǹkyé yɛ́ń.		May God give us a better tomorrow.

Exercises

1. Go outdoors and talk with your teacher and classmates about the prevailing weather conditions. Do you know what the weather will be like tomorrow? Discuss your guesses about the coming week's weather.

2. Based on your knowledge in weather conditions, fill in the blanks within the following sentences in Twi.

	Twi	English
a.	Ńsùtɔ́béré mú nó, _____ tɔ́ páá.	In the rainy season, it rains quite a bit.
b.	_____ àwìá m̀ḿɔ́ kὲsé.	The sun does not shine very much in the rainy season.
c.	Ǹsùó rὲtɔ́, ńsó _____wɔ̀ḿ.	It is raining, but the weather is hot.
d.	Ɔ̀pέbéré mú nó, _____fá páá.	During harmattan, the winds blow quite a bit.
e.	Àwìá ábɔ́, ńsó _____.	It is sunny, but I feel cold.
f.	Mὲpὲ àwɔ́ sénè _____.	I prefer cold to heat.
g.	Mὲm̀pὲ _____kóráá.	I don't like cold at all.
h.	Mὲǹhúù sέ _____ rὲtɔ́ dà.	I've never seen snow fall.

3. Say aloud and write the following in Twi:

  (a) It rained yesterday: _____

  (b) It is very warm today: _____

  (c) It is dry season in Ghana: _____

  (d) It does not snow in Ghana: _____

  (e) Where I come from, it is very cold: _____

  (f) What will the weather be like tomorrow? _____

4. Kyèrὲ àdéέ bàdkó á yὲyέ nò wɔ̀ ǹsútɔ́béré mú έné sέdèέyὲyέ nó.

13

At the Hospital – *Wɔ Àyàrèsábéá*

Generally, what happens in hospitals in Akan-speaking communities is the same as what happens in all parts of the world. Patients consult doctors about specific pains and ailments and doctors care for patients' problems. The first section of this chapter notes the Akan/Twi names of some parts of the human body (Credit: the image of the body come from Peter Kiselkov of Lance's Art Shack; http://artshack.webpark.sk/tutorials/body).

13.1 Parts of the body – *nìpàdùá sáákwá*

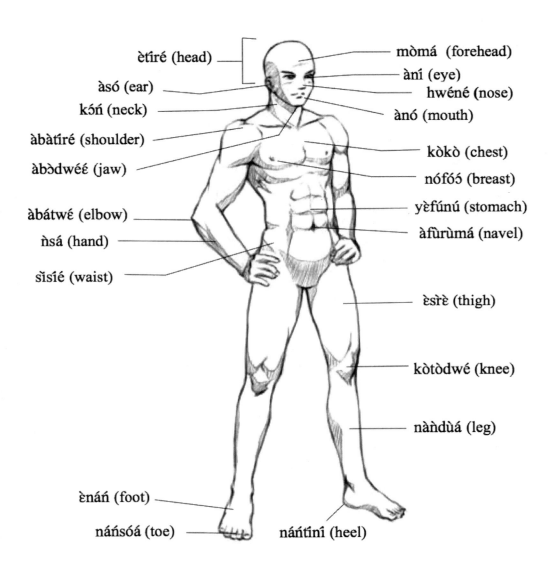

ètíré (head)

mòmá (forehead)

àní (eye)

àsó (ear)

hwéné (nose)

kɔ́ń (neck)

ànó (mouth)

àbàtíré (shoulder)

kòkò (chest)

àbɔdwéɛ́ (jaw)

nófóɔ́ (breast)

àbátwé (elbow)

yèfúnú (stomach)

ǹsá (hand)

àfùrùmá (navel)

sĭsíé (waist)

èsɾ̀ɛ̀ (thigh)

kòtòdwé (knee)

nàǹdùá (leg)

ènáń (foot)

náńsóá (toe)

náńtíní (heel)

Twi	English
àbàtíré	shoulder
àbátwɛ́	elbow
àbɔdwéɛ́	jaw
àdwéné	brain
àfónó	cheek
àkyí	back
àní	eye
ànìǹtɔ́ń	eyelash
ànó	mouth
àpàǹtáń	chin
àsó	ear
àtìkɔ́	back of the head
ètíré / ètí	head
ènáń	foot
ɛ̀séé	tooth
ɛ̀sɽ̀ɛ̀	thigh
ɛ̀tóɔ́	buttocks
hwéné	nose
kòkò	chest
kòtòdwé	knee
kɔ́ń	neck
mòmá	forehead
mɔ̀tòwáḿ	armpit
nàǹdùá	leg
náńsóá	toe
náńtíní	heels
ǹkàsɛ̀ɛ́	bones
ǹnwí	hair
nófóɔ́	breast
ǹsá	hands
ǹsátéá	fingers
ǹsáyáḿ	palm
ǹsònò	intestines
ǹtíní	veins
ɔ̀wèrɛ̀	nails
sìsíé	waist
tɛ̀kyèrɛ̀má / kɛ̀tèrɛ̀má	tongue
tíkwáńkùrá	skull
yɛ̀fúnú	stomach

13.2   Some diseases and physical disabilities – *ǹyàrèwá àhóròɔ́ bí*

Twi	English
àkòmàyáréɛ́ / mògyàbr̀òsòɔ́	heart attack / hypertension
àkyàkyà	hunch-back
ànìdáné	retroverted/tipped uterus
ànìfìrá	blindness
ànìsòbíré	dizziness
àsíkyìrèyáréɛ́	diabetes
àtírìdìí / fíbà	malaria / fever
àwósóɔ́	Parkinson's disease
àyàm̀túó	running stomach / gastroenteritis
àyɛ̀m̀bɔ́	diarrhea
àwɔ́	common cold
bàfáń	inability to walk / parapalegism
bòyíń	infertility
dwòdwóɔ́	stroke
dwòǹsɔ̀mógyá	syphilis
dwòǹsɔ̀yáá	gonorrhea
èkúró	sore
ɛ̀dáḿ	psychiatric illness / insanity
ɛ̀sóró	convulsion
ɛ̀té	cataract
ɛ̀twéré	epilepsy
ɛ̀wá	cough
gyèpìm̀	elephantiasis of the leg
hwènèmùsúó	runny nose
káká	tooth-rot
kòókó	piles / haemorrhoids
kɔ́m̀pɔ́	goitre
kɔ̀tèwúí	impotence
kr̀ótóá	asthma
kr̀òtòpɔ̀ń	tuberculosis
kwàtá	leprosy
mògyàwéɛ́	anaemia
m̀mùbúó	paralysis
múmú	deafness
ǹkwéé	hernia
ǹsàá	rashes
ǹwàáhónó	sore lips
pɔ̀m̀ɔ́	boil
tìpàéɛ́	headache
yàrèkòáńkr̀ɔ́ / bàbàsò wérɛ́m̀fóɔ́	A.I.D.S.
yɛ̀fùǹkéká	stomach-ache

13.3   Things to note at the hospital – *Ǹnéémá bí à yɛ́hú nò àyàrèsábéá*

Twi	English
àdúró	medicine
àgyààdwóɔ́	mourning
àhwɛ́	consultation
ámbùlànsè	ambulance
àpr̀éhyàè	operation
àsɛ̀m̀mìsá	question(ing)
àyàréfóɔ́	patients
èsúú	crying
m̀fìdíé	machines
m̀pá	bed
nɛ́ɛ̀sè	nurse
ǹtèàmú	shouting
ǹkɔ̀m̀mɔ́	conversation
ǹsàsòɔ́	queue / line
ǹyìànòó	answer(ing)
òdùyɛ́fóɔ́	doctor
ɔyáá	pains
pánéɛ́	syringe

13.4   Some useful expressions at the hospital – *Ǹsɛ̀m̀kèká bí à èhíá wɔ́ àyàrèsábéá*

Twi	English
Mèyáré.	I'm sick.
Òdùyɛ́fóɔ́, mèpààkyéw̌, bòà mè.	Doctor, please, help me.
Wò hééfá ná ɛ̀yɛ́ wò yá?	At which part of your body do you feel pain?
M'àní só bìrí mé.	I'm feeling dizzy.
Mè hó nyìnáá yɛ́ mè yá.	I have pains all over my body.
Mà}àmé nɛ́ɛ̀sè, òǹtùmí ǹnà.	Nurse, he/she can't sleep.
Nòm̀/fà àdúró yèí.	Take this medicine.
Wòàyɛ́ nò àpr̀éhyàè m̀mèɛ̀ǹsá.	She/he has undergone three operations.
Nè hó bɛ́tɔ́ nó.	She/he will recover.

13.5 A dialogue about parts of the body and some diseases – *Ǹkɔmmɔ́díe bí à ɛ̀fá nìpàdùá sàákwá nè yàréɛ̀ àhóròɔ́ bí hó*

	Twi		English
Yàá:	Nà ádéń nà mòàním áyɛ́ bòsàbósàà séí?	**Yaa:**	Why do you all look so sad?
	Àsɛ̀m̀bɔ̀né bí wɔ̀ hó ànáá?		Is there some bad news?
Kùmá:	Àáné, nà ɛ̀ǹyɛ́ ásɛ̀m̀ kétéwá.	**Kuma:**	Yes, and it is not a small one (a small piece of news).
	Táwíá *yáréɛ́* nó mú yɛ̀ɛ̀ dèń ànɔ̀pá yí, ńtí yɛ̀dè nó kɔ̀ɔ́ *àyàrèsábéá*.		Tawia's *illness* became serious this morning, so we took him to *hospital*.
Yàá:	Éi! Nà òdùyɛ́fóɔ́ nó sé sɛ́ń?	**Yaa:**	Ai! But what did the doctor say?
	Òbɛ̀wú ànáá?		Is he going to die?
Àtá:	*Hmm!* Wɔ̀yɛ́ɛ̀ ǹhwèhwɛ̀mú wíé nó, àdùyɛ́fóɔ́ nó kyèrɛ́ sɛ́ Táwíá áyà *bàbàsò wérɛ́m̀fóɔ́* nó bì.	**Atta:**	Hmm! After their diagnosis (tests), the doctors said Tawiah has got HIV (AIDS sickness).[1]
Yàá:	Óò! Yèí ńyɛ́ ásɛ̀m̀pá kóráá.	**Yaa:**	Oh! This is not good news at all.
	Áféí, máhú dèɛ̀ ńtí áà nà Táwíá *yám̀* rétú sàá nó.		Now, I know why Tawiah was having a *running stomach*.
Àtá:	Àáné! Sɛ́ *àyàm̀túó* pìì sàá yɛ̀ yàréɛ́ nó áhyɛ́àhyɛ́ǹsódéɛ́ nó mú bààkó.	**Atta:**	Yes! A long period of *running stomach* like that is one of the symptoms of the disease.
Kùmá:	Àféí ńsó, òdùyɛ́fóɔ́ nó sé Tàwíá hó *ápɔ̀m̀pɔ́* pìì né nè *náń* hó àkúró nó kyèrɛ́ sɛ́ yàréɛ́ nó ádídí nó mú páá.	**Kuma:**	Also, the doctors said that the many *boils* on Tawiah's body and *sores* on his legs tell that the disease is very well developed in him.
Yàá:	Sɛ́dèɛ̀ áyɛ́ yí dèɛ̀ ánìdàsóɔ́ ńní hó bíó.	**Yaa:**	How it is now, there is no hope any more.
	Ǹnórá ánàdwó séí, ɔ̀bɔ̀ɔ́ *wá* sàá árá kòsíí àdèkyèé.		Yesterday in the night, for instance, he *cough*ed till morning.
Àtá:	Yèí dèɛ̀ wódí ká?	**Atta:**	Do you have to say it?
	Yàréɛ́ yèí dèɛ̀ sɛ́ ɛ̀bɔ́ wò áà ná ɛ̀kyèrɛ́ sɛ́ wó né ǹkwà átó ǹkwàǹtá.		If you are infected with this disease, then, it means you have no hope of life anymore.
Kùmá:	Àáné ó! Àdéɛ́ yí ànó ǹní ádúró m̀pó.	**Kuma:**	Oh yes! After all there is no medicine against it.
	Àféí ńsó, ɛ̀bɔ́ wò à *tìpàèɛ́* m̀pó tùmí kú wò.		Also, if you are infected even a *headache* can kill you.
Yàá:	Táwíá kóráá ɔ̀kɔ̀fáà yàréɛ́ yèí fìrìì hé?	**Yaa:**	From where at all did Tawiah get this disease?

---

[1] Note that this discussion should be seen purely as a culturally typical discussion in Ghana, and should not be judged in terms of medical accuracy. So, for example, HIV and AIDS are medically distinct conditions, but the same word may be used for either condition among some Twi speakers.

Kùmá:	Hwáń nà òníḿ?	**Kuma:**	Who knows?
	Nàńsó mègyé dí sὲ òyá fìrìì *pánéέ* mú.		But I believe that he got it from a used *syringe*.
Àtá:	Wókyéréέ séń, Kùmá?	**Atta:**	What do you mean, Kuma?
Kùmá:	Ǹtì móńníḿ?	**Kuma:**	So you don't know?
	Ná Táwíá fá àdùbɔ́né áà yέdé pánéέ yέ nó bì.		Tawiah used to do hard drugs through the use of syringes.
	Ὲbíá ɔné àfófórɔ́ kyὲὲ pánéέ bàakó.		May be he shared one syringe with others.
Yàá:	Sàá'á? Ὲnéὲ sέ ɔnó árá nà ɔáyέ nè hó.	**Yaa:**	Is that so? Then he did the harm to himself.
	Ǹní sέ yὲsú má nó.		We don't need to pity him.

Exercises

1. Sit in groups of 2-4 and see if you can identify some of the parts of the body to each other, in Akan.

2. Sit in groups of 2-4 and try to mention as many names of the diseases and physical disabilities that you can think of, in Akan.

3. In the following pictures, identify and write the illness that each person is suffering from:

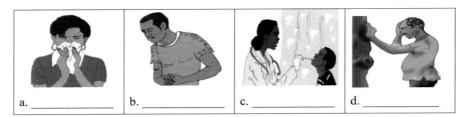

a. _____   b. _____   c. _____   d. _____

4. In the following pictures, identify the physical disability or profession of each person shown.

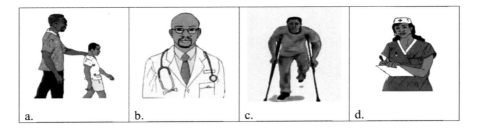

a. _____   b. _____   c. _____   d. _____

5. Say and write how you would tell the following sentences to a doctor in Twi.

Twi	English
a. _____	Please help me.
b. _____	I have a stomach-ache.
c. _____	I can't eat much.
d. _____	I'm feeling dizzy.
e. _____	Please give me medicine to take.
f. _____	My head has hurt all week.
g. _____	I think I have malaria.
h. _____	My mother had diabetes.

14

In the Drinking Bar – *Wɔ Ǹsàdwáásé*

Among the Akan-speaking peoples, drinking bars may be found just about anywhere provided there is enough space for people to sit and socialise. Traditionally, however, the best place for a drinking bar has always been under a big and well-shaded tree. This is because the trees provide a shelter against the sun in the afternoon. These days, buildings are put up for this purpose. One thing continues to define the traditional bars, though, which is the serving of indigenous or locally and traditionally brewed drinks. These days, one may also find Western drinks, which are either imported or locally brewed.

In the drinking bars, many events take place. It is normally a place for meetings, relaxation, fun, gossiping, socialisation, etc. Most of the time, there is also a lot of music and dancing. However, as in other places, people sometimes get drunk at bars, and so things can turn ugly. One might witness fighting, the trading of insults, etc. In the following we note some of the things one might find in a bar (both in local/traditional as well as modern bars).

14.1   Things to note – *àhyɛ̀nsòdéɛ́ bí*

Twi	English	Twi	English
ǹsá	drinks	sìgàréɛ̀tè	cigarette
ǹsátíré	cork	ǹsàbùèdéɛ́	opener
ǹsánóḿ	drinking	sìgàréɛ̀tènóḿ	smoking
àkònwá	chair	àbúá	smoking-pipe
àkònwàtéá	bench	dámè	draft
ɛ̀pónó	table	ɛ̀kòrá	calabash
ɛ̀tòá	bottle	àkététwúá	gourd
bètwàní	palm-wine tapper	kúrúwá	cup / glass
ǹkɔ̀m̀mɔ́	conversation	ǹnwóḿ	music
àkáńsíé	contests	àsá	dancing
kúkúó / àhèná	clay container	sàdwéàm̀	drunkard
m̀máá	females / ladies	m̀mèrémá	males / gentlemen
m̀mábáàwá	young ladies	m̀mèráńtéɛ́	young men
ǹtɔ̀kwá	quarrel / fight	ǹsékúró	gossip
báámàǹ	attendant	ǹwèwéɛ́	romance
gyáńtérà	prostitution	gyáńtéràní	prostitute

14.2   Kinds of drink – *ǹsá áhódóɔ́ bí*

Twi	English	Twi	English
bíyà	beer	pìtóò	millet-brewed wine
ǹsàfúfúó	palm-wine	àpètèhyì	palm-brewed alcohol
àdúsá	alcoholic bitters	dɔ̀ká	fermented palm-wine
bòbèsá	wine	ǹsàdɛ́	minerals (soft drinks)

14.3   Some useful expression at the bar – *Ǹsɛ̀m̀kèká bí à èhíá wɔ̀ ǹsàdwáásé*

Twi	English
Mà mè bíyà ǹkɔ̀tòá m̀mìènú.	Give me two bottles of beer.
Wóhìá (ǹsá) séń?	How many (drinks) do you need?
Màbórò yíé.	I'm very drunk.
Ǹsá nó ábà m'àní só.	I'm intoxicated.
M̀máá pìì ḿpé ǹsá áà ànó yé déń.	Most women don't like strong drinks.
Wò síká níé.	Here is your money.
Hwìè bòbèsá nó bí má mè.	Pour some of the wine for me.
Báámàǹ, fà nwóḿ bí sí só.	Attendant, put on some music.
Mà yéń ńní ásá / Mà yéń ǹsá.	Let's dance.
Àpètèhyì nà mèpé.	It is Akpeteshi that I like.
Tɔ́ ǹsá má mè.	Buy a drink for me.
Yɛ̀bénóḿ áwú.	We'll drink to death.

Ɔtɔɔ sìgàrɛ̀ɛ̀tè m̀mɛ́tɛ́m̀ náń.	He/she bought four sticks of cigarette.

14.4 A dialogue at the bar – Ǹkɔmmɔ̀díe wɔ ǹsàdwáásé

	Twi		English
Kwàdwó:	Báámáǹ, Sìtáà (bíyà bí) tòá bààkó yɛ̀ sɛ́ń?	**Kwadwo:**	Attendant, how much is a bottle of Star (a brand of beer)?
Báámáǹ:	Ɛ̀yɛ̀ sídì bààkó. Mɛ́m̀má wò sɛ́ń?	**Attendant:**	It is one cedi. How many should I give you?
Kwàdwó:	Mà mè ǹtòá m̀mìènú pɛ́, nà ǹnɛ́ dèɛ̀ àdwúmá áǹkɔ́ yíé.	**Kwadwo:**	Give me only two bottles, because today business was not good.
Báámáǹ:	Óò! Nà ǹnìpàdɔ́m̀ áà èdí w'àkyí yí dèɛ̀, sɛ́ m̀mìènú pɛ́ dèɛ̀ ńsò mó. Ànáá …	**Attendant:**	Oh! But with this bunch of people following you, two bottles will not be sufficient for you. Or …
Kwàdwó:	Mènìm sàá, ǹtì mà mè dèɛ̀ ànó yɛ́ hyé (àpètèhyì) nó tòá bààkó ńká hó. Né bóɔ́ dà só yɛ̀ m̀pɛ́séwá ádùòsíá nó árá?	**Kwadwo:**	I know that, so give me one bottle of the hot one (akpeteshi) in addition. Is the price still sixty pese-was a bottle?
Báámáǹ:	Àáné, ɛ̀bóɔ́ nó ńsésáè. Mè né wó yɛ́ àdwéné. Àpètèhyì dèɛ̀, wónúm̀ kàkŕá bí áà, ná wóábó.	**Attendant:**	Yes, the price hasn't changed. I agree with you. With Akpeteshi, even a little bit will get you drunk.
Kwàdwó:	Ɛ̀nó árá nà wóáká nó. M̀máá nó rénóm̀ pápá nó, ná m̀mèrímá nó ńsó gù kyèèhyéɛ́ nó só.	**Kwadwo:**	You have said it all. While the ladies are drinking the good one, we, the men, will be doing justice to the hot one.
Báámáǹ:	Nòkórɛ́! Mɛ́m̀fá ńkɔ́ mó pónó nó hó m̀má wó? Ànáásé wóárá wódè bɛ́kɔ́?	**Attendant:**	Right! Should I take them to your table for you? Or you will take them yourself?
Kwàdwó:	Óò! Wódè bɛ́kɔ́ ámà mè, nàǹsó mà mè sìgàrɛ́ɛ̀tè m̀mɛ́tím̀ ńsóń áǹsà, ná ká mé ká séèséí kyérɛ̀ mè.	**Kwadwo:**	Oh! You may send them for me, but before that, give me seven sticks of cigarette, and tell me how much I owe you as of now.

	Twi		English
Báámàǹ:	Mà mé ńhwέ.	**Attendant:**	Let me see.
	Sìgàrέὲtè nó bàakó yὲ mpέséwá núḿ, ǹtì wóká yέ sídì mmìènú né mpέséwá ádùòkŕóńnúḿ.		A stick of the cigarette is five pesewas, so your total cost is two cedis and ninety-five pesewas.
Kwàdwó:	Mèdàasè.	**Kwadwo:**	Thank you.
	Wò síká ní.		Here is your money.
Báámàǹ:	Kwàdwó, nà wóǹtɔ́ náḿ bíárá áǹká hò?	**Attendant:**	Kwadwo, but won't you buy any meat in addition?
Kwàdwó:	Dàabí! Mè hó sìká nyìnáá ásá.	**Kwadwo:**	No! I have no other money with me.
	Fà nwóḿ bí sí só má yὲǹ.		Put on some music for us.
Báámàǹ:	Yòò! Nwóḿ bέń nà wópέ?	**Attendant:**	All right! What music do you like?
Kwàdwó:	"Ɔ̀dɔ̀ yὲ dέ sénè sìká."	**Kwadwo:**	"Love is sweeter than wealth."
	Ɛ̀wɔ̀ Kwàdwó Áǹtwì ápáàwá fófórɔ́ nó só.		It is on the new album of Kwadwo Antwi.

14.5 A dialogue at the bar – *Ǹkɔ̀mmɔ̀díé wɔ̀ ǹsàdwáásé*

	Twi		English
Àgyèí:	Kwámè, nà wò hó tè sέń?	**Adjei:**	Kwame, how are you?
Kwámé:	Òǹyàmé ádóḿ ὲyέ.	**Kwame:**	By God's grace it is fine.
	Nà wó ńsóέ?		What about you?
Àgyèí:	Àà! ὲnyέ ḿpó á, yὲrὲkɔ̀ká ákyèrέ hwáń?	**Adjei:**	Ah! Even if it is not good, whom are we going to complain to?
Kwámé:	*Hmm!* Wóábísá ásέḿ páá.	**Kwame:**	Hmm! You've asked a good question.
Àgyèí:	Àháà, màté sὲ <u>Nàná kɔ́ àkùràà</u> (ɔ̀àwú).	**Adjei:**	Yeah, I've heard that the chief has <u>gone</u> <u>to the village</u> (he is dead).
	Ɛ̀yὲ nòkórέ?		Is that true?
Kwámé:	Éì! Ǹkɔ̀mmɔ́ bí séì dèè, sέ yὲdè ǹsánóḿ nà édíé óò!	**Kwame:**	Ai! Conversations like this have to go along with some drinks oo!
	Yέǹtùmí ḿfà y'ànì káń ńǹí.		We cannot talk about it in a sober state of mind.
Àgyèí:	Ɛ̀yὲ nòkwáré / nòkórέ.	**Adjei:**	It is true.

	Bètwàní, mà yèǹ ǹsàfúfúó nó kúkúó kὲséὲ bààkó, ná fá kòrá m̀mìènú ká hó bfà.		Palm-wine tapper, give us one big pot of palm-wine, and bring it along with two calabashes.
Kwámé:	Àháà! Àféí nà wórékásá sέ bὲrímá.	**Kwame:**	Aha! Now you are talking like a man.
B'ní:	Ǹsá nó né kòrá nó níé.	**Tapper:**	Here are the wine and the calabashes.
	Módè ká sídì náń pέ.		You owe me only four cedis.
Àgyèí:	Mèdààsè. Wò síká níé.	**Adjei:**	Thank you. Here is your money.
	Kwámè, yέńtwítwá bì ná fá dὲὲ ásíé bɔ́ mè.		Kwame, let us drink some and hit me with (tell me) what has happened.
Kwámé:	Ὲyὲ nòkóré. Nàná dàéέ áà, ɔànsɔré.	**Kwame:**	It's true. Chief went to bed and did not wake up (he is dead).
	Ǹkórɔfóɔ́ rèkèká sέ n'àkómàyáréέ nó nà ὲkúm̀ nó.		People are saying that it is his heart disease (hypertension) that killed him.
Àgyèí:	Àsὲm̀kὲséέ ábà ó!	**Adjei:**	We have a big issue at hand.
	Ńtí sèèséí ὲhé nà fúnú nó wɔ́?		So, where is the body now?
Kwámé:	Mègyé dí sὲ ὲwɔ̀ ǹkòǹwàfíésó sàá béré yí.	**Kwame:**	I believe that it is in the stool-house at this time.
Àgyèí:	Àà! Yέńtwέń ná yέńtíé dὲὲ m̀pànyìnfóɔ́ nó béká.	**Adjei:**	All right! Let us wait and listen to what the elders will say.
Kwámé:	*Hmm!* Mègyé dí sὲ έǹkyέ bíárá m̀pànyìnfóɔ́ nó dè bétó dwá.	**Kwame:**	Hm! I believe that the elders will announce it very soon.

Exercises

1. Say aloud the Twi names of some of the things one can find or see in a drinking bar. Don't forget to include people and activities as well as food and drink.

2. Say and write how you would ask the following questions at a drinking bar:

Twi	English
i. _____	Attendant, how are you?
ii. _____	What is your best drink?
iii. _____	What drink does your friend like?
iv. _____	How much does one beer cost?
v. _____	How much do I owe?
vi. _____	Do you have a good music?
vii. _____	What is your favorite kind of music?
viii. _____	Will the people be dancing?
ix. _____	Is that person drunk?
x. _____	Are you sober?
xi. _____	Would you like something to eat?
xii. _____	How are you feeling?
xiii. _____	Have you seen my friends?
xiv. _____	How can I call a taxi?
xv. _____	Won't you buy anything else?

3. Write the English names of the following Twi terms and associate each one of them with the appropriate picture below:

Twi	English		Twi	English	
ɛ̀kòrá	_____		àhèná	_____	
sàdwéàm̀	_____		àsá	_____	
sìgàrɛ́ɛ̀tè	_____		bíyà	_____	
ǹsánóḿ	_____		báámàǹ	_____	

15

Travelling: Twi for the Road – *Àkwántúó: Twì à Èhíá wɔ Kwáń mú*

In the olden days, the Asante people would walk (for short distances) or ride horses (for long distances) to get from one place to another. These days, there are several means people use to travel around in Ghana. However, it is not uncommon to find people walking for short or long distances, especially in rural communities where it is sometimes difficult to find motorised transport. In this chapter we explore some terms and expressions that are common and useful in travelling.

15.1 Things to note – *àhyɛ̀nsòdéɛ́ bí*

Twi	English	Twi	English
tìàséɛ̀nàm̀ / káà	car	mìrìká	running
tɔ́ɔ́rì	lorry	m̀pàbóá	shoes
tɛ́ɛ́sì	taxi	òfìdìkáfóɔ́ / dr̀ɔ́bà	driver
báàsè	bus	bòáfóɔ́ / máàtì	mate
ɛ̀hyɛ́ń	transport	twɔ́ɔ̀kò	choke / block
wìèm̀hyɛ́ń / ádúpèrè	aeroplane	kànéábògyá	traffic light
sùhyɛ́ń	ship	ǹnóɔ́má / ǹnéɛ́má	goods
pɔ̀ǹkɔ́	horse	ǹkɔ́bésíésó / ǹtwààhó	roundabout
dàdèpɔ́ńkɔ́ / sákìrè	bicycle / motor	twɛ̀m̀béá	crossing
nántéɛ́	walking	ǹkwàǹtá	junction
àgyìnàèɛ́ / gyìnábéá	station / stop	àkwàǹsíní	miles

15.2 Some basic terms in travelling – *àkwáńtúó mú ńsɛ́m̀ bí*

Twi	English
àkwáàbà	welcome
àmànèdíé	welcome proceedings
àmànèdéɛ́ / àmánéɛ́	something sent on an errand
àkwàǹsòdéɛ́	souvenir
ǹkr̀á	spoken message
ǹkr̀àdíé	farewell
bàábàyé	bye-bye
ǹkɔ̀mmɔ́	conversation

15.3 Some basic expressions in travelling – *àkwáńtúó mú ńkèkàé bí*

Twi	English
Ònyàmé né wó ńkɔ́.	May God go with you. / Safe journey.
Ònyàmé ńká wó hó.	May God be with you. / Safe journey.
Ònyàmé m̀fá wó ńkɔ́ m̀mr̀á.	May God see to your (safe) return.
Ònyàmé yɛ́ àdóm̀ áà …	God willing …
Nàntè yíé.	Walk well. / Farewell. / Goodbye.
Hwɛ̀ yíé.	Be careful / Take care.
Àkwáńgyá.	To see one off (in deed / in kind).
Ǹkyɛ́ bá.	Return soon.
Yɛ̀bɛ́fé wó. / Y'àfé wó.	We'll miss you. / We've missed you.
Yɛ̀bɛ́hwɛ́ w'ánìm̀.	We'll look forward to your coming.
Káà yèí rèkɔ́ hé?	Where is this car going?

Èfírí há rékɔ́ Kùmásé yɛ̀ sɛ́ń?	How much is it from here to Kumasi?
Àkwàǹsíní sɛ́ń?	How many miles?
Èfírí há rékɔ́ Kùmásé yɛ̀ àkwàǹsíní sɛ̀ń?	How many miles is it from here to Kumasi?
Mɛ́sáń (ábá).	I'll return. / I'll come back.
Méǹsáń (ḿmá).	I'll not return. / I'll not come back.
Fà fɔ́ḿ / Nàǹtè.	Walk (go on foot).
Fà káà.	Take a car (go by a car).
Twì / Kà káà.	Drive a car.
Tènà pɔ̀ǹkɔ́ só.	Sit on a horse.
Kà pɔ̀ǹkɔ́.	Ride a horse.
Twì dàdèpɔ́ǹkɔ́.	Ride a bicycle / motor.

15.4 Dialogues about travelling by road – *Ǹkɔ̀mmɔ̀díé bí à ɛ̀fá fɔ́ḿ àkwáńtúó hó*

Dialogue (1)

	Twi		English
Dúfíé:	Yàá, nà wò hó tè sɛ́ń?	**Dufie:**	Yaa, how are you?
Yàá:	Ònyàmé ádóḿ, ɛ̀yɛ́. Nà wó ńsóɛ́?	**Yaa:**	By God's grace, it is fine. What about you?
Dúfíé:	Ɛ̀yɛ̀. Wórèyɛ́ dééń wɔ Kégyétíá há ánɔ̀pá yí?	**Dufie:**	It is fine. What are you doing here in Kejetia this morning?
Yàá:	Mèrèbɛ̀fá lɔ́ɔ́rì àkɔ́ Sùàmè.	**Yaa:**	I have come to take a lorry to Suame.
Dúfíé:	Kégyétíá né Sùàmè dèɛ̀ sɛ́ wóbɛ́túmí ánàǹté ákɔ́. Ɛ̀ǹhìá sɛ́ wóbɛ́túá lɔ́ɔ́rì ká.	**Dufie:**	Between Kejetia and Suame, you can walk. You don't need to pay for a car.
Yàá:	Ɛ̀yɛ̀ nòkóré. Nàǹsó, mèrèpɛ̀ ǹtɛ́ḿ ǹtírá. Sɛ̀ mèrèbá áà, mɛ́fá fáḿ.	**Yaa:**	It is true. However, I'm in a hurry. When I am coming back, I will walk.
Dúfíé:	Yòò! Mé nsó mèrèkɔ́ hɔ́, ńtí mà yéńkɔ́ ḿmóḿ. Òfìdìkáfóó, bérɛ́ bɛ̀ń nà lɔ́ɔ́rì yí bétú?	**Dufie:**	All right! I am also going there, so let us go together. Driver, when will this lorry set off?
Dɽɔ̀bà:	Yɛ̀bétú sèèséí árá ǹtì mèpà mò kyɛ́ẃ móńfóró ná móńténá ásè.	**Driver:**	We will go very soon, so please get aboard and sit down.
Yàá:	Dúfíé, mà yéńténá ásè nà ɛ́ǹkyé ɛ̀béyɛ́ má.	**Yaa:**	Dufie, let us sit down because it will not be long to get full.

	Twi		English
Dṛɔ̀bà:	Àtó (bòáfóɔ́), yí twɔ́ɔ̀kò nó ná yéǹkɔ́.	**Driver:**	Ato (mate), take off the choke and let us go.
Dúfíé:	Dṛɔ̀bà nó ádì nòkwárɛ́.	**Dufie:**	The driver has been truthful.
	Ɔ̀àtú ǹtɛ́ḿ.		He has set off early.
	Máàtì, yèbésí wɔ̀ Àsɔ́réǹkwàntá.		Mate, we will get down at 'Asɔrenkwanta'.
	Yéǹ ká yɛ̀ sɛ́ǹ?		How much do we owe?
Máàtì:	Mèpààkyéẃ, sídì bààkó né m̀pɛ̀séwá àdùònù.	**Mate:**	Please, one cedis and twenty pesewas.
Dúfíé:	Wɔ̀ síká níé.	**Dufie:**	Here is your money.
	Gyè ná fá yɛ̀ǹ ǹsésá má yɛ̀ǹ.		Take it and give us our change.
Yàá:	Dṛɔ̀bà, mèpààkyéẃ gyìnà ǹkwàǹtá yí só ná yéǹsí.	**Yaa:**	Driver, please stop at this junction for us to get down.

Dialogue (2)

	Twi		English
Kùsí:	Ádɛ́ǹ nà ǹnípá pìì ábégú fíé há sàà?	**Kusi:**	Why have so many people come to this house?
Yàá:	Àdú rèkɔ̀ àbṛòkyíré, ńtí wɔ̀rèbèègyá nò kwáń.	**Yaa:**	Adu is going abroad, so they have come to see him off.
	Èbí ǹsó rèbèmàné wɔ̀ǹ àbúsùàfóɔ́ áà wɔ̀wɔ́ àbṛòkyíré hɔ́.		Others are also here to send something to their relatives abroad through him.
Kùsí:	Sàá? Àbṛòkyíré kùró bɛ́ǹ só nà wórékɔ́, Àdú?	**Kusi:**	Is that so? What foreign country are you going to, Adu?
Àdú:	Mèpààkyéẃ, mèrèkɔ́ mé pàpá hɔ́ wɔ́ Íngèlésì máń mú.	**Adu:**	Please, I'm going to my father in English country (i.e., Britain).
Kùsí:	Yòò! Ńtí wóbɛ́dí sɛ́ǹ wɔ̀ hɔ́?	**Kusi:**	All right! So, how long will you be there?
Àdú:	Médí bòsómé m̀mìènú pɛ́.	**Adu:**	I'll be there for only two months.
Yàá:	Àdú, káà nó áà ɛ̀dé wórékɔ́ Ǹkṛàǹ (wìèm̀kyéńgyínábéá) nó ábá, ńtí yɛ̀ nò ǹtɛ́ḿ.	**Yaa:**	Adu, the car that is taking you to Accra (the airport) has come, so hurry up.
Àdú:	Mèdààsé.	**Adu:**	Thank you.
	Nà wóńní ámànèdéɛ́ bíárá?		But don't you have anything to send?

	Wóńní àbùsùàní bíárá wɔ Íngèlési máń mú'?		Don't you have any relative in Britain?
Yàá:	Dàábí! Kyèà wó pàpá má yèǹ.	**Yaa:**	No! Send our regards to your father.
	Àféí ńsó, ká kyérὲ nò sέ wórèbá áà ɔ́ḿmáné yèǹ. Nàǹtè yíé.		Also, tell him to send us something when you're coming back. Goodbye.
Kùsí:	Bíò, sè wó pápá sέ yέń nyìnáá àfé nó páá.	**Kusi:**	Also, tell your father that we have all missed him.
	Ònyàmé né wó ńkɔ		May God go with you / safe journey.
Àdú:	Ɔbέté dèὲ móáká nó nyìnáá.	**Adu:**	He will hear all that you've said.
	Mé ńsó mέbŕέ mó Íngèlési máń mú ákwàǹsòdéέ.		I will also bring you souvenirs from Britain.
	Bàábàyé.		Bye-bye.
Òbíáá:	Ǹkyέ bá óó! Bàábàyééééé!!	**Everyone:**	Come back soon! Byeeeeeeeeee!!

Exercises

1. Pretend you're about to go on a journey. Explain in Twi to a friend why you have to take a bus or any other means of transport.

2. Your friend is travelling to Ghana. Have a short conversation with them about their journey, in Twi, using the dialogue above as a model. Be sure to appropriately greet your friend and bid farewell to your friend.

3. The following phrases in English are essential when going to a place you don't know. How will you say them in Twi?

Twi	*English*
a. _____	Can you go?
b. _____	Where is this bus going?
c. _____	Is this car going to town, please?
d. _____	Should I take a taxi or walk?
e. _____	How much is the fare from here to Kumasi?

f. _____ How many miles?

g. _____ Is it 2, 4 or 6 miles from here to town?

h. _____ I will not return soon.

4. One common way of getting around Ghana is by mini-bus, or *tro-tro*. Some Westerners consider the tro-tro to be an unsafe option for transportation. What do you think? Try to discuss your opinions on Akan as much as possible, using English only for words you've never learned.

16

Leisure time: Drumming and Dancing – *Àhóyábéré / Àhòmègyébéré: Twènèbɔ ́ né Àsá*

Drumming and dancing are characteristic and indispensable means of leisure in many, if not all, African societies. Among the Akan-speaking people, normally, after a hard days work, people often gather around and have fun through drumming and dancing. While some people may be drumming, others may be singing and dancing. Normally, it is the men who drum. The singing and dancing are also done by both men and women for a combination of tunes and entertaining group dancing.

Drumming and dancing are most typically seen in rural settings, but that does not mean that people who live in big cities do not also enjoy drumming and dancing. Urban Ghanaians often experience drumming through listening to recorded versions on machines at their homes, restaurants, and other public places of entertainment.

Among the Akan-speaking people, music can be found in almost all aspects of life. Even some occupations demand musical accompaniment for a favourable working environment and achieving good results. Music is often used to eliminate boredom in places where the work is particularly monotonous. Music is also used in occupations that demand physical strength, employed as a tool for soliciting collective effort. In some aspects of fishing and farming, for example, it is common to find people singing and drumming (but not necessarily dancing) as they work to entertain themselves and to keep their spirits up.

Drumming and dancing also take place during certain festive occasions, such as baby naming ceremonies (know as "outdoorings"), weddings, etc. At funerals and other solemn occasions, again, drumming and dancing play a significant role. In this chapter, we take note of some of the things that are associated with drumming and dancing.

16.1   Things to note – *àhyὲnsòdéέ bí*

Twi	English	Twi	English
nwóm̀	music	nwòn̄tòdéέ	instrument
nwòm̀tòfóɔ́	singer(s)	ὲdɔ́n̄	bell
twὲnéé	drum	àsá	dance / dancing
twὲnὲbɔ́	drumming	àtùm̀pán̄	kind of drum
twὲnὲbɔ́fóɔ́	drummer	àgórɔ́	game
àgòfóm̀má	members of a group	àbέn̄	trumpet / flute
sànkúó	organ / piano	mὲǹsón̄	animal horn flute
sànkùbɔ́fóɔ́	organist / pianist	àbòdùá	claves
fíríkyíwá	finger-worn metal block	dáwúró	single (big) cowbell
tòtòsánsán̄	twin cowbell	àkàsàá	rattle
àdòwá ,	kinds of drumming / music	èdwá	gathering
kὲtὲ,		èdwám̄	dancing floor / stage
high-life,		kɔ́tɔ́kórɔ́	7-shaped drum stick
sὲkyì, *etc.*		dòǹnó	talking drum

16.2 Pictures of some of the things associated with drumming and dancing – *Ḿfòyíní bí à èfá twènèbɔ́ né àsá hó*

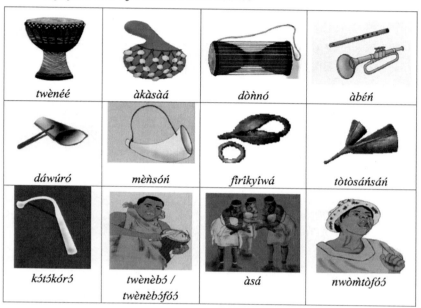

twènéé	*àkàsàá*	*dònnó*	*àbéń*
dáwúró	*mènsóń*	*firíkyíwá*	*tòtòsáńsáń*
kɔ́tɔ́kórɔ́	*twènèbɔ́ / twènèbɔ́fóɔ́*	*àsá*	*nwòm̀tòfóɔ́*

16.3 A dialogue about drumming and dancing – *Ǹkɔmmɔ́díe bí à èfá twènèbɔ́ né àsá hó*

	Twi		English
Òsèé:	Àdò, twènéé béń nà wóníḿ bɔ́?	Osei:	Ado, what drum do you (know how to) play?
Àdò:	Mènìm pìì bɔ́, nànsó mèbɔ́ *dònnó* yíé páá. Nà wó ńsóɛ́?	Ado:	I know how to play many of them, but I play *donno* very well. What about you?
Òsèé:	Mènníḿ èmú bíárá bɔ́, nànsó mèpè nó tíé páá.	Osei:	I dont know how to play any of them, but I like to listen to them a lot.
Yàá:	Ǹtì, wóńníḿ nwòm̀déé bíárá bɔ́?	Yaa:	So, dont you know how to play any instrument?
Òsèé:	Mènìm firíkyíwá bɔ́ kàkŕá.	Osei:	I know how to play *finger-wear metal block* a little.
Yàá:	Fíríkyíwá dèè sɛ́ m̀mɔ̀fŕá m̀pó nìm̀ bɔ́. Àsá ńsóɛ́?	Yaa:	As for *finger-wear metal blocks*, even children know how to play it. What about dancing?
Òsèé:	Mèpè àsá páá. Ǹkrɔ̀fóɔ́ m̀pó ká sɛ̀ mèsá *kètè* (mà né yɛ̀) fɛ̀ páá.	Osei:	I like dancing a lot. People even say that I dance *kete* beautifully.

Àdò:	Ḿmáá pὲ àsá yíé, ńtí mὲgyé dí sὲ Yàá ńsó nìm̀ ásá.	**Ado:**	Women like to dance very much, so I believe Yaa also knows how to dance.
Yàá:	Ááné! Mènìm̀ *àdòwá* nὲ *sὲkyì* sà páá. Sùkúù mú ńsó, mèsùá sàǹkúó né àbéń bɔ́.	**Yaa:**	Yes! I know how to dance *adowa* and *sɛkyi* very well. At school, I also learn how to play organ and flute.
Àdò:	Ὲyέ! Wó né Òsὲé nyìnáá ním *kὲtὲ* sà yí dὲὲ, ɔkyéná móbέsá ámà yὲàhwέ wɔ́ ɔhéné ádwábɔ́ nó àsé.	**Ado:**	Good! Since you and Osei know how to dance *kete*, tomorrow you will dance for us to see at the chief/kings gathering.
Òsὲé:	Èí! Èdwáṁ sàà dὲὲ méńtùmí ǹsá.	**Osei:**	Ai! On such a floor, I cannot dance.
Àdò:	Óò! Ὲǹyέ hú sàà. Àgòfóṁmá nó bέbɔ́ kété ámà ǹnípá pìì àsí dwàṁ, ńtí ὲnó árá né sέ wóáfŕá mú.	**Ado:**	Oh! It is not that frightening. The (music) group will play *kete* for a lot of people to get on the floor, so you just have to join in.
Òsὲé:	Yòò! Mέbɔ́ ḿmɔ́dέń ásá. Yàá, nà wó ńsóέ?	**Osei:**	All right! I will try to dance. What about you, Yaa?
Yàá:	Mèṁfá hó. Wósá áà, mé ńsó mέsá.	**Yaa:**	I don't care. If you dance, I will also dance.

Exercises

1. Do your personal hobbies include music or dancing? Tell your classmates, in Twi, about those hobbies. If you're not very musical, describe the instruments, songs, or dances you might be interested in learning more about.

2. In Twi, tell your friends some things about drumming and dancing in Akan-speaking cultures. What instruments do Ghanaians use that are the same or different as the instruments in your culture?

3. With the help of your instructor, try to sing some songs in Twi! Learning and memorizing songs is one great way to remember some Twi words for many years to come, so work on dedicating at least one song to memory. Ask your instructor about the history of the song(s) he/she teaches you.

4. Try to learn one particular Ghanaian dance (e.g. *Kete*) from your teacher. What are the leg and the hand movements involved? Describe them in Akan-Twi to the best of your ability.

17

At a Funeral – Wɔ Àyíéásé

The Akan people have a long and detailed process of funeral celebrations. Right from the time a person dies, plans are put in place for his/her funeral. A funeral may go on for a year with particular days set aside for the remembrance of the deceased. Besides the actual date that is set aside by the family for the actual funeral when one dies, a week, forty days, and one year after the death is also commemorated.

   The funeral officially starts when the body is prepared and laid in bed overnight and officially ends after the family has sat down (in an outdoor gathering), after the burial of the deceased, for sympathizers to come and express their sympathies. In the expression of sympathy, people give contributions (in cash or in kind) towards the recouping of the running cost of the funeral and other expenses (*e.g.*, the welfare of the deceased's children).

Generally, the Asantes, Akuapem, and Fantes bury their dead rather than choose cremation, except in particular cases, such as if it was the wish of the deceased to be cremated. During the funeral, people normally wear black or red clothes to signify that they are in mourning. Those close to the deceased also wail a lot, as an indication of their loss. Through chanting, some others also recount the life and some of the good deeds of the deceased.

Although it is generally a sorrowful event, as one of the rites of passage of Akan-speaking peoples, a funeral is also seen as a celebration of the life of the deceased. This is especially true if the deceased died a normal or honourable death and at an old age. Thus, besides the crying and mourning, family members of the deceased and sympathizers often have fun as well by drinking, eating, singing, drumming and dancing. Where the deceased was a very old person, people normally wear white clothes to signify thanksgiving to the gods. This chapter covers some of the terms and expressions that are associated with death and funerals in Ghana.

17.1   Things to note – *àhyɛ̀nsòdéɛ́ bí*

Twi	English	Twi	English
èsúú	crying	òwúó	death
àgyàadwóɔ́	wailing / mourning	fùǹdáká	coffin
yàadíé / àmìadíé	mourning	kùnàfóó	widow(er)
nwómtóɔ́	singing	àmáńnéɛ́	ritual
ǹtèàtèàmúú	shouting	àgyàǹká	fatherless
àpɛ́síé	wake-keeping	àwísíá	orphan
àsá	dancing	àfúnú / àmú	corpse
àkɔ́ḿkyéné	fasting	nwóḿ	music
ǹsánóḿ	drinking (alcohol)	àsìèɛ́	cemetery
bèsèwéɛ́	chewing cola	àníbŕɛ́	seriousness
ǹsá	drinks	àmànèhúnú	suffering
àwèrɛ̀hóɔ́	sorrow	nàwótwédá	one week celebration
àwèrɛ̀kyékyé	sympathy	àdàdùànáń	fortieth day celebration
bìrísì	black cloth	àfédá	one year celebration
kɔbéné	red cloth	frígyì mú	inside a fridge (mortuary)

17.2   Indirect ways to announce death – *Àkwáń áhódóɔ́ à yɛ̀fá só ká sɛ̀ òbí áwù*

Twi	English
Ɔkɔ́ nè kŕá ákyí.	She/he has gone behind her/his soul.
Ɔkɔ́ àkùràá.	She/he has gone to the village.
Ɔkɔ́ nè ǹsámàǹkyíré.	She/he has gone behind his ghost.
Ɔàdá nè béńkúḿ só.	She/he has slept on her/his left.
Ɔàtwá n'àní áhwɛ̀ dáń.	She/he has turned her/his face towards the wall.
Ɔdàé áà ɔ̀àǹsɔ̀ré.	She/he went to bed and did not wake up.
Ɔné àtèàsèfóɔ́ átwà mú.	She/he has cut ties with the living.

Ɔné àtèàsèfóɔ́ átò ǹkwàǹtá.	She/he has parted ways with the living.
Ɔàyé Nyàmé déá.	She/he has become God's property.
Ɔàtòà nànánóḿ.	She/he has followed the ancestors.
Ɔàyé sámáń.	She/he has become a ghost.
Ɔàgyáé mú.	She/he has given up.
Ɔàgyáé ńkwá mú.	She/he has given up on life.
Ɔàtɔ́.	She/he has fallen.
Ɔàká àkyéné ágú.	She/he has thrown off salt.
Ɔàká n'ànó átò mú.	She/he has shut (her/his mouth) up.

17.3 Some basic expressions about death and funeral – *Ǹkèkàé bí à ɛ̀fá òwúó né àyíé hó*

Twi	English
Sìèsìè fúnú nó.	Prepare the corpse.
Dèdà fúnú nó.	Lay/put the corpse in bed.
Sìè fúnú nó.	Bury the dead.
Yɛ̀rèdí n'àdàdùànáń.	We are celebrating his/her 40th day of death.
Kùnàfóɔ́ nó rèdí àwèrɛ̀hóɔ́.	The widow(er) is sorrowful.
Ǹyàǹká nó rèsú.	The orphans are crying.
Ɔrètwá àgyààdwóɔ́.	He/she is wailing.
Mèwɔ́ yààdíé. / Àmìàdíé mú.	I'm in mourning.
Mɛ̀fúrá bɛ̀rísì.	I have put on *brisi*.
M'àní ábré.	I'm serious.
Yɛ̀wɔ àyíé mú.	We are in a funeral.
Òwúó m̀pɛ́ sìká.	Death does not like money.
Òbíárá bɛ́wú.	Everyone will die.
Òwúó ńyɛ́ ǹyìyì mú.	Death does not discriminate.
Òwúó ńníḿ pàníń ànáá àbɔ̀frá.	Death does not know an adult or a child.
Yɛ̀rèkyérè kɔ́ḿ.	We're fasting.
Òwúó tírí mú yɛ̀ déń.	Death is wicked.
Òwúó yɛ̀ nípá m̀fásòɔ́.	Death is the benefit of mankind.

17.4   A dialogue about a funeral – Ǹkɔmmɔdíe bí à ɛ̀fá àyíé hó

	Twi		English
Àfúá:	Ádéń nà òbíárá résú rètéátèà mú sàà?	**Afua:**	Why is everybody crying and shouting like that?
Àdò:	*Hmm!* Àsɛ̀m̀ kɛ́séɛ́ bí ábà.	**Ado:**	Hmm! We are faced with a big issue.
	Sèèséí árá nà yènyáá ǹkr̀á sɛ́ Àtàá ádá nè béńkúm̀ só.		We just got information that Ataa is dead.
Àfúá:	Óò! Ná ɔyàré ànáá?	**Afua:**	Oh! Was she sick?
Àdò:	Mèǹnìm déɛ́.	**Ado:**	I don't know.
	Ɔáwú yí dèɛ̀, sɛ́ ná ɔyàré óò ná ɔǹyàré óò ɛ́ńyɛ́ ásɛ́m̀ bíó.		Now that she is dead, whether she was sick or not doesn't matter any more.
Àfúá:	Ɛ̀yɛ̀ nòkórɛ́.	**Afua:**	That is true.
	Mà yɛ̀m̀pɛ̀ br̀ísì bí m̀fírá, ná yéńkɔ́má kùnàfóɔ́ nó né n'àbúsùàfóɔ́ dùé.		Then, let us look for some *br̀ísì* to wear and go to sympathize with the widower and his family.
Àdò:	Yòò! Màwíé.	**Ado:**	All right! I am done.
	Wó ńsó wóáwíé áà, mà yéńkɔ́.		If you are also done, let us go.
Àfúá:	Àbúsùàfóɔ́, yɛ̀mà mò yàákɔ́.	**Afua:**	Family members, accept our condolences.
	Dùé né àmànèhúhú.		Sorry for this painful incident.
Àfóɔ́:	Yɛ̀dà mò àsè.	**Family:**	We thank you.
	Àkwáàbà ǹsó!		Also, welcome!
	M̀pànyìǹfóɔ́ sɛ́ yɛ̀nìm̀ ńsó yèbìsá.		Elders say we know, but we ask anyway.
	Nà àmàǹnèɛ́?		So, what brought you here?
Àdò:	*Hmm!* Yɛ̀àté àsɛ́m̀ áà ásí nó.	**Ado:**	Hmm! We have heard what has happened.
	Yɛ̀bàà sɛ́ yɛ̀rèbɛ̀má mó dùé, ná yéátíé àyíé nó hó ńhyèhyɛ̀ɛ́ áà móáyɛ́.		We came to sympathize with you and to find out about the plans you have made about the funeral.
Pànyíń:	Ɛ̀ǹné ǹnáwɔ́twé, yèbédí ǹnàwɔ́twédá nó.	**Elder:**	We will perform the "week's rituals" a week from today.
	Yɛ̀béyɛ́ àyíé nó ánkásá ńsó bòsómé áà ɛ̀rébá yí dá áà ɛ̀tɔ́ só núm̀.		We will also celebrate the actual funeral on the fifth day of the coming month.

Àdò:	Yòò! Ńtí móbédédà nò ànáá (módè nó bétó ḿpá mú ànáá)?		**Ado:**	All right! So, would you lay the body in bed?
Pànyíń:	Àáné! Yèdè àmú nó bétó ḿpá mú ásì pé.		**Elder:**	Yes! We will lay the corpse in bed and keep a wake.
	Àféí, ànòpá hó bààbí, ná yèàkósíé.			Then, somewhere in the morning, we will go and bury it.
Àfúá:	Nà ǹwísíá (òwùfóó nó ḿmá) nó wò hé?		**Afua:**	So, where are the orphans (the deceased's children)?
Pànyíń:	Wòń né wóń nànàbáá wò dáń mú hó.		**Elder:**	They are in the room with their grandmother.
	Òkùnàfóó nó ńsó né ǹnípá kó Kùmásé.			The widower has also gone to Kumasi with some people.
Àfúá:	Kùmásé dèè wòrèkò yé dééń wò hó?		**Afua:**	What are they going to do in Kumasi?
Pànyíń:	Wòdè àmú nó rèkò kyé fŕígyì mú.		**Elder:**	They are going to put the corpse (in the fridge) at the mortuary.
	Wòbésáń ńsó áhyè fùǹdáká.			They will also make an order for a coffin.
Àdò:	Yòò! Énèè, yèbékó.		**Ado:**	All right! Then, we will go.
	Òkùnàfóó nó bá áà móńkyéá nó ḿmà yéń.			Send our condolences to the widower when he comes.
À'fóó:	Yòò! Yèdà mò àsè né ǹsrá.		**Family:**	All right! We thank you for the visit.
	Yèbéhwé mó áníḿ ǹnàwótwé sé ǹné.			We will look forward to your coming next week.
Àdò:	Sédèè ètéé bíárá móbéhú yéń.		**Ado:**	You will definitely see us.
	Nyàmé né mó ńténá.			May God be with you.
	Óńhyé mò dèń ǹsó.			May He also strengthen you.

Exercises

1. Write down five expressions used to report death in Akan-Twi:

   (a) _____

   (b) _____

   (c) _____

   (d) _____

   (e) _____

2. Memorize and say aloud at least three expressions which are announced in Akan-Twi when someone dies.

3. In your opinion, why do you think Ghanaians from Akan-Twi speaking cultures chose to express death in these ways, instead of reporting death in more clear (*i.e.*, literal or explicit) terms? Give two reasons, in Twi if you can, otherwise using English.

4. Imagine you are at a funeral. List five things or events that you readily observe to your classmates/friends, in Akan.

18

Flora & Fauna – *Àfîfîdéɛ̀ nè Ḿmóádómá*

Ghana is a beautiful country with a highly diverse selection of plants and animals. In this chapter you will get to know the Akan-Twi names for some of these. Since Ghana, like other West African countries, lacks vast conservation areas and huge herds of wildlife found in other parts of Africa, some of the the creatures listed here may be more likely to be found in Ghanaian stories, myths, and legends, rather than daily life. One exception to this is Mole National Park, located in Northern Ghana. Other animals listed here may be unfamiliar to you, but are quite commonly found in Akan-speaking communities in Southern Ghana, such as the 'grasscutter' (also known as the Greater Cane Rat), a very large rodent whose meat is considered a delicacy.

18.1 Some plants and animals – àfìfìdéɛ̀ nè m̀móádómá bí

Twi	English	Twi	English
túró	garden	àdòwá / wàǹsàné	antelope
àfúó	farm	ànòmàá	bird
wíráḿ / ɛ̀pɔ́ḿ	forest	dábòdábò	duck
wírá / wúrá	weeds	àkɔ̀m̀fɛ́ḿ	guinea fowl
èdùà	tree	ákó	parrot
ǹhwíré	flowers	àfàfàǹtɔ́	butterfly
ǹtíní	roots	àkókɔ́	chicken
kòòkóò	cocoa	kr̀ókr̀ókòkò	turkey
m̀mìré	mushroom	pr̀ɛ́kó	pig
àhàbáń	leaf	nàǹtwíé	cow
ápáń	bat	pàtúó	owl
ɔ̀kr̀á	cat	àpɔ̀ǹkyé	goat
kr̀ámáń	dog	àpɔ̀ǹkyébá	kid (baby goat)
sàkr̀ámáń	wolf	òdwáń	sheep
ɔ̀wɔ́	snake	òdwáńbá	lamb
ɔ̀sónó	elephant	gyàtá	lion
sèbɔ́	tiger	àdwéné	fish
sùsónó	hippopotamus	mɔ́ǹkɔ́	shrimp
kótérɛ́	lizard	dɛ́ńkyɛ́ḿ	crocodile
àdàǹkó	rabbit	kúsíé	bush rat
àkr̀àǹtéɛ́	grasscutter	àkùrá	mouse
àpɔ̀ǹkyèrèní	frog	àkyèkyèdéɛ́	tortoise
ǹtétéá	ants	ɛ̀nwá	snail
tɛ́fŕɛ́	cockroach	èdwíé	lies
àkɛ̀ɛ́tíá	chimpanzee	àdwéé	monkey
kɔ́tɔ́	crab	àhyéẃ	baboon
ǹtóńtóḿ	mosquito	pɔ̀ǹkɔ́	horse
pétɛ́	vulture	kwàákwàádòbí	crow
òpúró	squirrel	nwáńséná	housefly

18.2 Some plants in pictures – àfìfìdéɛ̀ bí ḿfónní

| ǹhwìré | àhàbáń | dùá | m̀mìré |

18.3 Some animals in pictures – *m̀móádómá bí m̀fónínί*

ǹtétéá	*kŕámáŋ́*	*àdàǹkó*	*pŕékó*
sὲbɔ́	*ɔ̀sónó*	*àpòǹkyé*	*òdwáŋ́bá*
ɔ̀wɔ́	*ànòmàá*	*pàtíió*	*àkókɔ́bá*
àkɔ̀ǹfέḿ	*sàkŕámáŋ́*	*dábòdábò*	*àdwéné*
àpòǹkyὲrὲní	*òpúró*	*àkùrá*	*ákó*
ɔ̀kŕá	*gyàtá*	*pɔ̀ǹkɔ́*	*déŋ́kyéḿ*

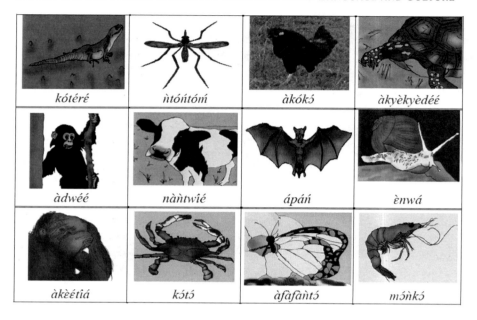

kótéré	*ǹtóńtóḿ*	*àkókɔ́*	*àkyèkyèdéé*
àdwéé	*nàǹtwíé*	*ápáń*	*ɛ̀nwá*
àkɛ̀étíá	*kɔ́tɔ́*	*àfafaǹtɔ́*	*mɔ́ǹkɔ́*

18.4 A dialogue about plants and animals – *Ǹkɔmmɔ́díe bí à ɛ̀fá àfìfìdéɛ̀ nè ḿmóádómá hó*

	Twi		English
Àfúá:	Àdú, wóáhù àkɛ̀étíá dà?	**Afua:**	Adu, have you seen a chimpanzee before?
Àdú:	Dààbí! Àdɛ́ń nà wórébísá mè?	**Adu:**	No! Why are you asking me?
Àfúá:	Wó nà wótáá kɔ́ wíráḿ.	**Afua:**	It is you who usually go into the forest.
	Ɛ̀nó éńtí nà mèrébísá wò nó.		That is why I am asking you.
Àdú:	Ɛ̀yɛ́ dèǹ sɛ́ wóbɛ́hú àkɛ̀étíá wɔ̀ bààbí áà mékɔ́ nó.	**Adu:**	It is hard to see a chimpanzee where I go.
	Wɔ̀táá wɔ́ kwáéɛ́ mú páá.		They are usually in the deep forest.
Àfúá:	Sàá? Nà ḿmóá bí tè sɛ́ wàǹsàné né n'àséfóɔ́ nóḿ ńsóɛ́?	**Afua:**	Is that so? What about animals like antelope and related ones?
Àdú:	Wɔ́ń ḿpó gyésɛ̀ ànàdwò.	**Adu:**	Even with them, it is only in the night.
	Ɛ̀nó éńtí nà ánàdwó nà mè táá kɔ́ àháyɔ́ nó.		That is why I usually go hunting at night.
Àfúá:	Màhú sɛ̀ wówɔ̀ ǹnwáń, ḿpɔ̀ǹkyé nè ǹkókɔ́ pìì.	**Afua:**	I have seen that you have many sheep, goats and chicken.
	Àdɛ́ń éńtí nà wókɔ́ àháyɔ́ ńsó?		Why do you also go hunting?
Àdú:	Ɛ̀nyɛ́ àháyɔ́ títíré ńtí nà mèkɔ́ wíráḿ.	**Adu:**	Hunting is not the main reason why I go into the forest.

	Mèkɔ́ kɔtwá ǹhàhàmá áà mè m̀pɔ̀nkyé nè ǹnwáń nó béwé.		I go to get the leaves that my goats and sheep will feed on.
Àfúá:	Yòò! Mé ńsó mérèkɔ́ áfúó mú ákɔbú ńnùá kàkŕá, ná máhwɛ̀ ńsó sɛ̀, m'àfídíé áyì àkràntéɛ́ bí ànáá.	**Afua:**	All right! I am also going to the farm to cut some trees and also check to see if my trap has caught any grass-cutter.
Àdú:	Yòò! Wónyà àdàⱥgyé áà tètè ǹkòǹtómìré kàkŕá brɛ̀ mè, mèpààkyéẃ.	**Adu:**	All right! If you have time get me some cocoyam leaves, please.
Àfúá:	Yòò! Mététè bí ábrɛ̀ wó. Ɛ́ǹnèɛ̀ méhú wò àkyíré yí.	**Afua:**	All right! I'll get you some of those. I will see you later then.

Exercises

1. Say aloud the Akan words for all the plants and animals. Which ones are your favourites? Discuss, in Akan. Practice using colour terms and other descriptive words you know.

2. Using the list of animals' names listed in this chapter, group them into wild and domestic animals.

3. Make sentences or create a conversation about some of the plants and animals you now know, in Akan.

e.g.	*Gyàtá hó yɛ̀ hú páá.*	'A lion is very frightening.'
	Mèwɔ̀ ǹkŕámáń m̀mìènú.	'I have two dogs.'

a. _____ _____

b. _____ _____

c. _____ _____

d. _____ _____

e. _____ _____

19

Government & Politics – Àbán né Àmànyɔsɛ̀m̀

Ghana gained independence from the British on March 6, 1957, and became a republic on July 1, 1960. Before independence, Ghana was called the Gold Coast (or *Sìkámpòànó* in Twi). Ghana is under a democratic rule.

The country consists of 10 regions and 230 electoral constituencies. The 10 regions are Asante, Brong Ahafo, Central, Eastern, Greater Accra, Northern, Upper East, Upper West, Volta, and Western (see the map in Chapter 6). Each region is headed by a politically appointed regional minister, but all of them are governed by the central government. Each constituency may consist of districts and each district is headed by a politically appointed District Chief Executive (DCE). Each constituency is also represented in parliament by a parliamentarian who is elected by people from that constituency.

19.1 Things to note – *àhyɛ̀nsòdéɛ́ bí*

Twi	English
àbáń	government
ǹkábóḿábáń	union government
ɔ̀máń	country
ɔ̀máḿbá / àmáfóɔ́ / àmáḿḿá	citizen / citizens
àmàǹfráfóɔ́ / ànànàfóɔ́	foreigners
àmáḿmúó	governance
m̀pàsóá	constituent
m̀pàsóásó	constituency
bɾɔ̀nóó	area
máńtáḿ	region / state
máńsíní	district
èkùró	town
èkúó	group / organization / institution / society
àmáńyɔ́ / àmàǹyɔ̀sɛ́m̀	politics / politicking
àmàǹyɔ̀kúó	political party / organization
àmàǹyɔ̀sɛ́m̀	matters relating to politics
àmàǹyɔ̀ní	politician
ɔ̀màǹpànyíń	head of state / president
dádá	old / past / Ex-
àbèdìàkyíré	vice- / deputy-
ɔ̀màǹpànyíń àbɛ́dìàkyíré	vice-president
ɔ̀màǹpànyíń dádá	ex-president
àgyìnàtúó	council
àgyìnàtúfóɔ́	members of a council
ɔ̀máńágyínàtùfóɔ́	members of council of state
àsòèèyɛ́	ministry
sòáfóɔ́	minister
m̀mèrá	law
bédwá	assembly / gathering
m̀mɾàhyɛ́	law-making
m̀mɾàhyɛ́bédwáḿ	parliament
m̀mɾàhyɛ́bédwàní	parliamentarian
m̀mɾàhyɛ́bédwáḿkásàmáfóɔ́	speaker of parliament
kà-bí-ḿmá-mé-ńká-bí	democracy (lit: say something, let me say something)
òbí-ńká-bí	dictatorship (lit: no one says anything else)
ɔ̀twèrɛ́fóɔ́	secretary
ɔ̀kásáfóɔ́	spokesman
àbá	vote / seed

tó	to vote; to throw
àbátóɔ́	voting / elections
àbátóɔ́ áfé só	voting age
dódóɔ́	majority
kétéwá / kúmáá	minority
kùdódóɔ́	majority group
kùkétéwá	minority group
dódóɔ́ áfá	majority side
kétéwá áfá	minority side
fàahódíé	independence

19.2   Some ministries of government – *àbáń mú àsòèèyɛ́ bí*

Twi	English
sìkàsɛ́ḿ né àhòsìèsíè	finance and economic planning
ɔ̀máń hó báḿbɔ́	defense
ɔ̀máń mú báńbɔ́ / àfísɛ́ḿ	interior
àmànòné ńsɛ́ḿ	foreign affairs
m̀m̀ràkyɛ́bédwáḿ ńsɛ́ḿ	parliamentary affairs
dwádíé né m̀fìdìdwúmá	trade and industry
èfíéhwɛ́ né ǹkùràséé ńkɔ́sóɔ́	local government and rural development
àdèsúá	education
m̀máábúnú né àgórɔdíé	youth and sports
àdùàné né kùàyɔ́	food and agriculture
ǹnwúmá né àtènàèé	works and housing
àpòmùdéń	health
àhòɔdéń	energy
àsàsé, kwáéɛ́ né fàm̀tútúó	lands, forestry and mines
àbɔ́déɛ́-mú-ńhwèhwèèé,	science, environment and technology
ɔ̀bɔɔ̀àdéɛ́bɔ́bré né sùàhúnú fófórɔ́	ogy
m̀máá né ǹkwàdàá ńsɛ́ḿ	women and children affairs
ǹkùtàhòdíé	communications
dàwùbɔ́ / àmànèèbɔ́	information
àgyìnàèé, àkòràèé né kétékékwáń	ports, harbours and railways
nípá áhòɔdéń né àdwúmáyɛ́	manpower and employment
àkwáń, àkwàǹtènpɔ̀ń né ɛ̀kyéń	roads, highways and transport
ànkóréánkóré ńnwúmá ńkɔ́sòɔ́	private sector development
ɔ̀máńbáńbɔ́ hó fòtúfóɔ́	national security advisor
pɛ́pɛ́ɛ́pɛ́yɔ́ né kámáfóɔ́	justice and attorney general

19.3 A dialogue about government and politics – *Ǹkɔmmɔ̀díe bí à ɛ̀fá àbáń né àmàǹyɔ̀séḿ hó*

	Twi		English
Àfúá:	Yàẁ, ɔmàǹpànyíń kóráá n'àdwúmá né sɛ́ń?	Afua:	Yaw, what at all is the work (or responsibilities) of the president / head of state?
Yàẁ:	Óò! Ɔmàǹpànyíń dèɛ̀ sɛ́ n'àdwúmá árá né ɔmáń yí ńkɔ́sóɔ́ só hwɛ́ né àmáḿfóɔ́ hó báń bɔ́.	Yaw:	Oh! As for the president, his job is mainly to see to the development of this country and the protection of its citizens.
	Ádɛ́ń ɛ́ńtí nà wórébísá mè sàá		Why are you asking me that?
Àfúá:	Ɔwɔ̀ àsòàfóɔ́ pìì.	Afua:	He has many ministers.
	Ńtí ɛ̀yɛ́ mè sɛ̀ ɔ̀ǹyɛ́ hwèè.		So, it seems to me that he does nothing.
Yàẁ:	*Ha ... ha!* Ɛ̀ńté sàá.	Yaw:	Ha ... ha! It's not so.
	Ɛ̀wɔ̀ḿ sɛ́ àsòàfóɔ́ nó nà ɛ̀yɛ́ ǹnwúmá nó déɛ́, nàǹsó ɔmàǹpànyíń nà ɔhwɛ́ wɔ̀ń nyìnáá só.		It is a fact that the ministers do the work, but it is the president who supervises all of them.
Àfúá:	Yòò! Ɛnó ńtí nà ɔmàǹpànyíń nó árá yí àsòàfóɔ́ à ɔné wɔ̀ń bú ɔmáń nó?	Afua:	Alright! Is that why the president himself appoints the ministers he wants to rule with?
Yàẁ:	Àáné! Sɛ̀ wóhwɛ́ áà, àmáńfóɔ́ nà wɔtó àbá yí ɔmàǹpànyíń.	Yaw:	Yes! If you look at it, it is citizens who vote to elect the president.
	Nàǹsó, àsòàfóɔ́ déɛ́, yɛ̀ntó ábá ǹyì wɔ́ń.		But, as for the ministers, we do not vote to elect them.
Àfúá:	Ɛ́ńtí àsòàfóɔ́ nó ńní àkòǹtàbúó bíárá bú kyèré yɛ̀ǹ, ɔmáńfóɔ́, nó ànáá?	Afua:	So, aren't the ministers accountable to us, the citizens?
Yàẁ:	Wɔwɔ̀ àkóńtá bú kyèré yéń.	Yaw:	They are accountable to us.
	Ɛ́ńtí nà áǹsáná òbí béyɛ́ sòáfóɔ́ nó m̀m̀ràhyɛ́bédwáfóɔ́ bí fíífìì nó nó.		That is why before someone becomes a minister he/she is vetted by some parliamentarians.
Àfúá:	Wóákáé mé. Hwáń nà òtúmí gyíná sɛ́ m̀m̀ràhyɛ́bédwání?	Afua:	You have reminded me. Who can stand as a parliamentarian?
Yàẁ:	Ɔmàḿbá bíárá àà ɔ́ádú àbátóɔ́ áfé só nó tùmí gyìná sɛ́ m̀m̀ràhyɛ́bédwání.	Yaw:	Any citizen who has reached voting age can stand as a parliamentarian.
Àfúá:	Ɛ̀sɛ̀ sɛ́ ɔdɔ́m̀ àmàǹyɔkúó bí àǹsà ànáá?	Afua:	Does he/she have to join a political party?
Yàẁ:	Dààbí! Òbí bétúmí ágyìná fààhódíé / àṅkórɛ́áṅkórɛ́ só ɛ́wɔ̀ nò m̀pàsóásó.	Yaw:	No! Someone can stand independently (*i.e.*, without any party affiliation) at his/her constituency.
Àfúá:	Sàá?	Afua:	Is that so?

	Ǹtì Gáánà yàá fàahódíé yí, m̀pɛ́ sɛ́ń nà yɛ́átó àbá áyí ɔ̀mànpànyíń?	So, since Ghana became independent, how many times have we voted to elect the president?
Yàẁ:	Àmànpànyíń áà yɛ́átó àbá áyí wɔ́ń yɛ́ nàń.	**Yaw:** Presidents who we have voted to elect are four in number.
	Nàǹsó, yàtó àbá m̀pɛ́ ńsìá.	But we have voted six times.
Àfúá:	Ádɛ́ń ńtí(rá)?	**Afua:** Why is that?
Yàẁ:	Ɛ̀fìrì sɛ́ yɛ́átó àbá áyì wɔ̀ǹ mú m̀mìènú m̀prènú.	**Yaw:** Because we have voted to elect two of them two times each.
	Mà mé m̀mísá wò bì.	Let me ask you something.
	Kà-bí-m̀má-mé-ńká-bí àbáń né òbí-ńká-bí àbáń; èmú dèɛ̀ wɔ́ hé nà wópɛ́?	Democratic government and dictatorial government; which one of them do you prefer?
Àfúá:	Mè dèɛ̀, mèpɛ̀ kàbí-m̀má-mé-ńká-bí àbáń.	**Afua:** As for me, I like democratic government.
Yàẁ:	Yòò! Yɛ̀m̀fá ǹkɔ́m̀mɔ́ nó ńsí há.	**Yaw:** Let us end our conversation here.
	Àkyíré yí yɛ̀bɛ́tóá só.	We will continue some other time.

Exercises

1. Answer the following questions in Twi:

   (a) In the absence of the president, who takes charge of affairs?

   _____

   (b) If *fíé* means 'house' in Twi and *ǹkòǹwàfíé* means 'stool house', how do we say parliament house in Twi?

   _____

   (c) Supposing you are the ex-vice president of Ghana, how will we refer to you in Twi?

   _____

   (d) What do we call the minister of defence and interior, in Twi?

   _____

2. Translate the following English sentences about government and politics into Akan:

   (a) Dictatorship is not a good system of government.

   _____ .

   (b) My father is a politician.

   _____ .

   (c) She works at the Ministry of Youth and Sports.

   _____ .

3. Translate the following Twi sentences about government and politics into English:

   (a) *Gáánà* rètó àbá ǹnɛ́.

   Ghana _____ today.

   (b) Kàbí-ḿmá-mé-ńkábí àbáń yɛ́ páá.

   _____ .

   (c) M̀m̀ràhyɛ́bèdwàní *bíárá* ká nòkwáré.

   Every _____ .

4. Discuss—in Twi if you can, otherwise in English—what questions you may still have about the way politics and government works in Ghana. How are things different in comparison to your native country?

20

Law & Order – *Ṁmèrá né Ǹhyèhyɛ̀ɛ́ɛ́*

Law and order is kept by the government through the judiciary and the security services in Ghana, in a similar manner as in many other countries. The security service consists of the army, the police, the courts, the prisons, etc. In this chapter, we note some terms and expressions relating to law and order.

20.1   Things to note – *àhyɛ̀nsòdéɛ́ bí*

Twi	English
ǹnyìnàsòdéɛ́ / ṁmŕáńnyínàsòɔ́	constitution
ǹsɛ́ḿsíɛsíébéá	judiciary / judicial service
àsɛ̀ńníbéá / àsɛ̀ńnìɛ́ɛ́	court
àsɛ̀ńnìpɔ̀ń	supreme court
àsɛ̀ńnìpɔ̀ń ábédìàkyíré	high court
àsɛ̀ńsìsòɔ́díbèá	appeal court
àtɛ́ń / àtɛ́ḿmúó	judgement
ɔtɛ̀ḿmùáfóɔ́	judge
bɔné	crime
bɔnèyɛ́fóɔ́	convict (the person convicted)
bɔnèyɛ́fóɔ́ dádá	ex-convict
àtɛ̀ńkyìà	bad / wrong judgement

ɔ̀kàsàmáfóɔ́ / ɔ̀kámáfóɔ́	lawyer
àdáńséɛ́	witness
àdáńsèdíé	witnessing
àdáńsèkúrúmú	false witnessing
àdáńsèdéɛ́	evidence / exhibit
ɔ̀kàm̀fóɔ́	accused / defense
àsɛ́m̀tósóɔ́	accusation
ǹtwátósóɔ́	wrong accusation
háẃká / sé	complaint / report
háẃkáfóɔ́ / séfóɔ́	complainant
ɔ̀sr̀áàní / sógyà	soldier
pòlíísì / pòósì	police
dèdùàní	prisoner
dèdùàfíé / àfíásé	prisons / jail / cells
pòǹkyíré	counter-back
àbáńkàbá	handcuffs
àtúó né àkòǹtíbàá	guns and sticks
bím̀	victory / innocent / not guilty
fó	loss / guilty
ǹsɛ̀m̀mìsá	questioning
ǹsɛ̀m̀fóó	nonsense
ànóyíé / m̀mùàyé	answering / reply
àtɛ́m̀múó ábòáfóɔ́	jury (*lit*: helpers of judgement)
kóńtóḿpótwá	lying
ǹsámáń	sue
ǹsámáń krátàá	warrant
àgyìná	stand
bùà	to give a sentence
kúm̀fó	to be on death row
m̀pátá	compensation
máńsóó / màǹsòtwé	litigation
màǹsòtwéní	litigant

20.2 Some statements relating to law and order – *Ǹsɛ́ḿ bí à ɛ̀fá m̀m̀rá né ǹhyèhyɛ̀ɛ́ hó*

Twi	English
Wò ànìmùòyáḿ.	Your honour.
Mé wùrà.	My lord.
Mèdí bìm̀.	I am innocent (not guilty).
Ǹtwá kóńtóḿpó.	Do not lie.
Yɛ̀í yɛ̀ àtɛ̀ǹkyèá.	This is a wrong/unjust judgement.
Òbí dè àsɛ́ḿ átò mè só.	Someone has accused me (of doing wrong).
Ǹtwátósóɔ́ yɛ̀ yá.	Wrongful accusation is painful / It is painful to be wrongfully accused.
Mèrèsàmáǹ àbáń.	I am suing the government.
Yɛ̀àbúá àbȓáńtéɛ́ nó kúḿfò.	The young man has been sentenced to death.
Ɔ̀tɛ̀m̀mùáfóɔ́ nó ábù àtɛ̀àntèné.	The judge has delivered a just judgement.
Àpòósìfóɔ́ bɔ́ yɛ̀ǹ hó báń fírì ǹnìpà ábɔ̀néfóɔ́ hó.	The police protect us from bad people.

20.3 A dialogue about law and order – *Ǹkɔ̀mmɔ̀díe bí à ɛ̀fá m̀m̀rá né ǹhyèhyɛ̀ɛ́ hó*

	Twi		English
Àfúá:	Mèrèkɔ̀fá àsȓáàfóɔ́ ámà wóábɛ̀kyé Yàẁ.	Afua:	I am going to get soldiers to come and arrest Yaw.
Àkúá:	Ádɛ́ń? Yàẁ àyɛ́ wò déɛ́ń?	Akua:	Why? What has Yaw done to you?
Àfúá:	Ɔ̀àdídí mè àtɛ́ḿ.	Afua:	He has insulted me.
	Àféí ńsó, ɔ̀àbɔ́ m'àsóḿ.		And, also, he has slapped me.
Àkúá:	Óò! Nà sɛ́ yɛ̀í dèɛ̀ ǹyɛ́ àsȓáàfóɔ́ àsɛ́ḿ.	Akua:	Oh! But this is not a matter for soldiers.
	Ɛ̀sɛ̀ sɛ́ wókɔ́ ká kyéɾɛ́ àpòósìfóɔ́ m̀móḿ.		You have to report/complain to the police rather.
Àfúá:	Ádɛ́ń ńtí nà ńyɛ́ àsȓáàfóɔ́ àsɛ́ḿ?	Afua:	Why is it not a matter for soldiers?
Àkúá:	Àsȓáàfóɔ́ àdwúmá né ɔ̀máń hó báńbɔ̀, ǹyɛ́ ánkóɾéánkóɾé ńsɛ́ḿ bí tètè sɛ́ wó dèɛ́ yí.	Akua:	The responsibility of soldiers is the protection of a country, but not taking care of individual cases like yours.
Àfúá:	Màté. Mèrèkɔ̀ àpòósìfóɔ́ ásóɛ́ɛ́ ákɔ̀ká mé háẃ ná médè àpòósìfóɔ́ ábà sèèséí árá.	Afua:	I have heard you (Alright). I am going to the police station to report my case and come with the police very soon.
Àkúá:	Àfúá, mà nó ńká.	Akua:	Afua, let it be.

	Ḿmá m̀mèrá ḿfá Yàẁ ǹkɔ̀tó áfíásé.		Don't let the law send Yaw to prison.
Yàẁ:	ɛ́déɛ́ń nà mó ḿmîènú rédí hó ńkɔ̀mmɔ́ yí?	**Yaw:**	What are you two talking about?
Àkúá:	Àfúá sé ɔrèkɔ̀fá àpòósìfóɔ́ ámà wóábɛ̀kyɛ́ wó.	**Akua:**	Afua says she is going to get the police to arrest you.
Yàẁ:	Àfúá, (nà) màyɛ́ wò déɛ́ń?	**Yaw:**	Afua, (but) what have I done to you?
Àfúá:	Wò wérɛ̀ àfí sɛ́ wóyéyɛ́ɛ̀ mé bóbɔ́ɔ̀ m'àní só ànɔpá yí?	**Afua:**	Have you forgotten that you insulted me and slapped me this morning?
Yàẁ:	Mɛ̀pà}àkyéẃ, yèí dèɛ̀, mà yɛ́ńká nò fíé. Àkúá, kà bí má mè.	**Yaw:**	I beg you, this one, let us talk about it at home. Akua, plead on my behalf.
Àkúá:	Àfúá, wóde kɔ́ àpòósìfóɔ́ ásóɛ́ɛ́ áà, sɛ́dèɛ̀ ɛ̀téé bíárá ɛ̀bɛ́kɔ́ àsɛ̀ǹníbéá ná àkɔ́yɛ́ àsɛ́ḿ téńtéń.	**Akua:**	Afua, if you take it to the police, by all means, it will go to the court and turn into a far-reaching issue.
Àfúá:	Ɛ́ńtì déɛ́ń?	**Afua:**	So what?
Àkúá:	Ɛ́ńtì mà yɛ́ńsíésíé àsɛ́ḿ yí wɔ̀ há yí árá. Yèí, àkámáfóɔ́ né ɔtɛ̀m̀mùáfóɔ́ bíárá hó ńhìá.	**Akua:**	So let us settle this case right here. For this one, lawyers and a judge will not be necessary.
Yàẁ:	Ènhìá ḿpó sɛ́ yɛ̀bɛ́ká nò téńtén bíárá. Mèdí fò. Àfúá, mɛ̀pà}àkyéẃ fá kyɛ́ mè.	**Yaw:**	It is not necessary for us to spend too much time talking about it. I am guilty. Afua, I beg you, forgive me.
Àfúá:	Màté àséɛ́. Mède àkyɛ́ wó. Ɛ̀ǹyɛ́ sàá bíó.	**Afua:**	I have understood. I have forgiven you. Do not do that again.
Àkúá:	Yɛ̀dàásé. Méhyɛ́ Yàẁ só ámà nó ápàtá wó.	**Akua:**	We thank you. I urge Yaw to compensate you.

Exercises

1. Translate the following English sentences about law and order into Twi:

(a) Every country <u>has</u> a constitution. :

_____wɔ _____ .

   (b) The man has sued me. :

   _____ .

   (c) Lawyers talk <u>for</u> us. :

   _____má _____ .

2. Translate the following Twi sentences about law and order into English:

   (a) Gáánàfóɔ́ pɛ̀ màǹsòtwé páá :

   Ghanaians _____ .

   (b) Ádɛ́ń ńtí nà Yàẁ dá áfíásé? :

   _____ .

   (c) Yèí ńyɛ́ ásɛ́ḿ. :

   This _____ .

3. Write the answers to the following questions in Twi.

   (a) Who defends an accused in court? :

   _____ .

   (b) How is the judge referred to during submissions? :

   _____ .

   (c) Who pleads guilty or not guilty in court? :

   _____ .

   (d) What do we call a person who is into litigation? :

   _____ .

21

Applications and interviews – *Ǹhwèhwɛ̀ɛ̀ɛ́ né mú Ǹsɛ̀m̀mɩ̀sá*

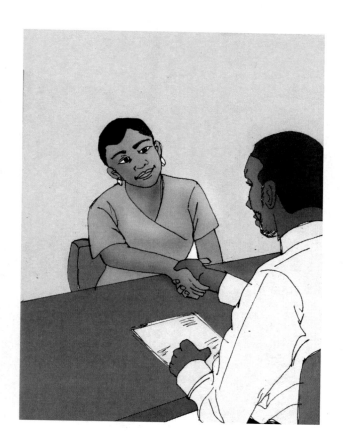

21.1 Some jobs and positions – ǹnwúmá né àdìbérέ bí

Twi	English	Twi	English
ɔtwèrὲtwéréfóɔ	secretary	ɔtὲmmùáfóɔ	judge
séséfóɔ	accountant	ɔkámáfóɔ	lawyer / advocate
sìkàkóráfóɔ	banker	ɔsràání	soldier
àdèpàmfóɔ	tailor / seamstress	hwèhwὲmfóɔ	investigator / detective
òtùmfóɔ	blacksmith	káfóɔ	operator
m̀fòyìm̀twáfóɔ	photographer	hwὲsófóɔ	foreman
m̀mràhyέbèdwàní	parliamentarian	títénání	chairman
kìrùfásà / òdìyífóɔ	magician	yíkyéréfóɔ	actor
twèréfóɔ	writer / typist	ɔkàndìfóɔ	leader / manager
kwàǹkyèréfóɔ	director	òdùyέfóɔ	doctor
òdíyífóɔ	prophet	òdùkyéréfóɔ	pharmacist
ɔkyèrὲkyéréfóɔ	teacher	òdùyέfóɔ bóáfóɔ	nurse
dwàdìní	trader	ɔkyèrέmúfóɔ	translator
ɔsófó	priest	òkùàfóɔ / òkùàní	farmer
kɔm̀fóɔ	fetish priest	ɔfàréfóɔ	fisherman
àsὲm̀pàkáfóɔ	evangelist	ɔsèǹkàfóɔ	broadcaster
sàm̀fóɔ	editor	ɔsὲǹtwèréfóɔ	journalist
ɔbíḿfó	professor	pààdìfóɔ	labourer
ɔhémáá	queen	ɔhéné	chief / king
sùání	student /disciple	nwòm̀tòfóɔ	singer
fìrìkáfóɔ / dìrɔbà	driver	sòáfóɔ	minister of state
èfíémbòáfóɔ	domestic helper	bàm̀bɔfóɔ	security/body guard
àdùànènúáfóɔ	caterer	àbɔ́déέḿhwàhwέfóɔ	scientist
fòtúfóɔ	advisor / councillor	ɔkyèàmé	linguist / master of ceremony
hwὲsófóɔ	caretaker	ǹsὲǹkwààyífóɔ	joker / comedian
gyáńtéràní	prostitute	káyá(ní)	carrier

21.2 Some statements about jobs – Ǹsέḿ bí à ὲfá ǹnwúmá hó

Twi	English
Mèyέ sùání.	I am a student/disciple.
Àsɔ́fó ádwúmá yὲ dèǹ.	The work of priests is difficult.
Yàréfóɔ bíárá hìá òdùyέfóɔ.	Every sick person needs a doctor.
Ɔhéné bíárá yὲ déhyéέ.	Every king /chief is a royal.
Àkùàfóɔ hó hìá wɔ ɔmáń mú.	Farmers are important in a country.
Àtwèrὲtwéréfóɔ tàá yὲ m̀máá.	Secretaries are often females.
Gyáńtéràbɔ́ yὲ àníwú.	Prostitution is embarrassing.
Àdwàdìfóɔ m̀pέ sέ wɔbέbɔ́ ká.	Traders do not like to make loss.
Mèpὲ sέ mèyέ òdùkyéréfóɔ.	I want to be a pharmacist.

21.3 A dialogue about applications and interviews – *Ǹkɔ̀mm̀ɔ̀díe bí à ὲfá ǹhwὲheὲὲὲ né mú ǹsὲm̀mìsá hó*

	Twi		English
Àtàá:	Màkyé, Òwúrà! Mè díń dè Àtàá Máńsá.	Ataa:	Good morning, Sir! My name is Attaa Mansa.
Òwúrà:	Yὲὲnùá! Wórèhwèhwέ hwáń?	Sir:	Good morning! Who are you looking for?
Àtàá:	Mèrèhwèhwέ Òwúrà Bàá, ɔkàǹdìfóɔ́ nó.	Ataa:	I am looking for Mr. Baah, the leader/manager.
Òwúrà:	Yòò! Wó né nó wɔ ǹhyèkyὲὲέ?	Sir:	Alright! Do you have an appointment with him?
Àtàá:	Àáné!	Ataa:	Yes!
Òwúrà:	Twὲǹ kàkŕá, mèpàkyéẃ. Ὲsὲ sέ mèká kyéré nò sέ wóábá.	Sir:	Wait for a while, please. I need to tell him you are here.
Àtàá:	Yòò!	Ataa:	Alright!

...After some time – *m̀mŕέ kàkŕá ákyí*

	Twi		English
Òwúrà:	Òwúrà Bàá sέ bŕà mú.	Sir:	Mr. Baah says come in.
Àtàá:	Mèdàsè!	Ataa:	Thank you!
Òwúrà:	Yèǹní ásèdá.	Sir:	Not at all (You're welcome).
Àtàá:	Màkyé, ɔkàǹdìfóɔ́!	Ataa:	Good morning, manager!
Ɔ'fóɔ́:	Màkyé, Wóbétúmí átènásé. Mègyé dí sὲ àdwúmá hó ǹsὲm̀mìsá nó ńtí nà wówɔ́ há?	Manager:	Good morning! You may sit down. I believe you are here for the job interview?
Àtàá:	Mèpàkyéẃ, àáné!	Ataa:	Please, yes!
Ɔ'fóɔ́:	Wóáyὲ sèséfóɔ́ ádwúmá pέń?	Manager:	Have you worked as an accountant before?
Àtàá:	Mèpàkyéẃ, àáné! Màyέ sèséfóɔ́ m̀féέ núḿ wɔ Gáánà sùkúùpɔ́ń mú.	Ataa:	Please, yes! I have been an accountant for five years at the University of Ghana.
Ɔ'fóɔ́:	Nà ádέń ńtí nà wórépέ àdwúmá fófórɔ́?	Manager:	But why are you looking for a new job?
Àtàá:	Nòkwáré ní àkàtùá áà mègyé wɔ hɔ́ nó sòà.	Ataa:	Truthfully, the salary I take there is meagre.

	Àféí ńsó, mèrèhwèhwé sùàhúnú fófóró.		Also, I am looking for new experience.
Ɔ'fóɔ́:	Wóákásá yíé. Màhwɛ́ wò ǹkɾátáá mú.	**Manager:**	Well said. I have looked into your particulars.
	Mègyé dí sɛ̀ wófàtà àdwúmá yí.		I believe you deserve this job.
Àtàá:	Mèdàásè! Yɛ̀í kyèɾɛ́ sɛ́ màyà àdwúmá nó ànáá?	**Ataa:**	Thank you! Does that mean I have the job?
Ɔ'fóɔ́:	Ɛ́èbía! Ɛ̀sɛ̀ sɛ́ mè né àdwúmá yí mú ḿpànìmfóɔ́ bí dwénè hó ànsáànà màtùmí ákà sɛ́ wóáyá àdwúmá nó ànáásɛ́ dàábí.	**Manager:**	Maybe! I need to discuss it with some leaders of this company before I can say whether you have a job or not.
Àtàá:	Yòò!	**Ataa:**	All right!
Ɔ'fóɔ́:	Mèdàásè sɛ́ wóbáà ǹsɛ̀ḿmìsá yí. Wóbɛ́té yɛ̀n ǹká ànìmàníḿ yí áɾá.	**Manager:**	Thank you for coming for this interview. You will hear from us very soon.
Àtàá:	Mè ńsó mèdàásè. Ɛ́nèè, mɛ́sɾɛ́ kwáń ákɔ.	**Ataa:**	Thank you too. In that case, I will ask for your permission to leave.
Ɔ'fóɔ́:	Ɛ̀kwáń dà hó. Nàǹtè yíé.	**Manager:**	Permission granted. Safe journey.

Exercises

1. Try to respond to the following questions about application and interview in Twi.

Question	Response in Twi
a. Good afternoon!	_____
b. Who are you looking for?	_____
c. Have you taught before?	_____
d. Why don't you like your present job?	_____
e. What makes you good for this job?	_____
f. *Wóbɛ́gyé àkàtùá sɛ́ń?*	_____

2. Identify and write down the profession/job of the following people in Twi.

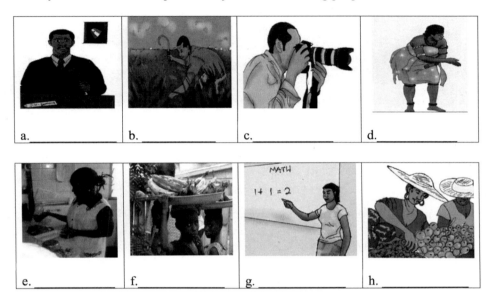

a. _____ b. _____ c. _____ d. _____

e. _____ f. _____ g. _____ h. _____

3. Would you be interested in working in Ghana? If so, what profession would you like to pursue? What concerns do you have about finding such work? Discuss these interests and concerns to the best of your ability, in Twi.

Appendix A

Facts to note in pronunciation – *Ǹnéɛ́má títìré bí áà ɛ̀wɔ́ kàsàéɛ́ mú*

A.1 Vowel harmony

Vowel harmony is one of the most important rules to observe in the pronunciation of Twi words. The rule is, however, not very obvious in the orthography as some of the vowels—i.e., /ɑ, ʊ, ɪ /—are not used in the standard orthography. In other words, these vowels are just phonetically significant. Together, the vowels are divided into two main sub-groups with regards to the advance tongue root (or 'ATR') specifications. These are advanced and unadvanced sub-groups:

Advanced	[+ATR]	[i, e, ɑ, o, u]
Unadvanced	[−ATR]	[ɪ, ɛ, a, ɔ, ʊ]

The ATR rule in Twi requires that, in a word, only vowels from one set of the two vowel groups must appear, as shown below. As also shown below, there are a few words that violate the rule though, having vowels from both sets, but these words are considered as having a *two-span harmony*, instead of a violation.

	Orthographic	*Phonetic*	*Gloss*
+ATR	afidie	ɑfidie	'a trap/machine'
+ATR	abomuu	ɑbomuu	'stew'
−ATR	abɔsoɔ	abɔsʊɔ	'a belt'
−ATR	sɔneɛ	sɔnɪɛ	'a sieve'

Two-span

aduane	[ɑduanɪ]	'food'
nyinsɛn	[nyinsɛɪ]	'pregnancy'

A.2 Other properties

Tone

Akan-Twi is a tone language with two-tone levels: H (high) and L (low). This is shown in the tables below, and is marked throughout all Twi examples in this book. Twi also has a downstepped-H tone, in both words and phrases, also as shown below, which is marked with a ! symbol before the syllable with the downstepped tone.

If you don't already speak a tone language, mastering your own production of the tones will take some practice. The best way to learn to perceive and produce downstep is to listen to a native speaker pronounce these words aloud and in contrast to one another in order. It's also best to listen and identify these tones in isolation (*i.e.*, just reading the examples below) and in context (*i.e.*, asking a native speaker to use each word in a few different sentences).

	L			*H*	
pàpà	'fan'		pápá	'good'	
prà	'to sweep'		néέmá	'goods'	
hòmè	'to breathe'		káká	'tooth-rot'	
tènàsè	'to sit down'		bɔ́tɔ́	'a sack'	
kàsà	'to talk'		sɔ́m̀	'worship'	

	LH			*HL*	
pàpá	'father'		dúkù	'scarf'	
àbòfrá	'a child'		káà	'a car'	
sìká	'money'		tíkyà	'teacher'	
tòá	'a bottle'		sófì	'shovel'	
sèbɔ́	'a tiger'		táyà	'catapult'	

Lexical downstep

àdá!ká	'a box'
ká!sá	'language'
bέ!yíé	'witch'
ɔbɔ́!fóɔ́	'a messenger or an angel'

Non-lexical downstep

mè	+ kὲté	'I + mat'	→ mè kέ!té	'my mat'	
àsέm̀	+ ká	'story + to say'	→ àsέm̀!ká	'evangelism'	
yàréέ	+ m̀pá	'sickness + bed'	→ yàrém̀!pá	'a sick bed'	
Kòfí	+ Àtá	'Kofi + Atta'	→ Kòfí Á!tá	'Kofi Atta'	

Nasalization

The vowels in Akan may also be classified into high /i, ɪ, u, ʊ/; mid /e, ɛ, o, ɔ/; and low /ɑ, a/. All the high and low vowels can have nasal counterparts for phonemic distinction, shown below, and all the high vowels are also nasalized before a nasal consonant, as also shown here:

	Non-nasalized		*Nasalized*
ka	'bite'	kã	'to say/tell'
fi	'to get out'	fĩ	'dirt'
fɪ	'to vomit'	fĩ	to cause to happen
esu	'character'	esũ	to cry
dwʊm	'to get cold'	dwʊ̃	to harvest a yam

Some other words with nasalization

hwĩm	'to take away unexpectedly'
sĩma	'a minute'
sũm	'to push / to support'
dwʊ̃	'to reduce the brightness of a lamp'

Nasal homorganism

In Twi and Akan in general, the nasal phoneme (represented here as *N*) occurring before other consonants adopts the place of articulation of these succeeding consonants. This process is called homorganic nasal assimilation or nasal homorganism. The illustrations here show the various allophonic representations of the nasal, as dictated by place of articulation of the consonant that follows it. In some dialects of Akan, including Asante Twi, if the the consonant that follows the nasal, *N*, is voiced, then it also becomes a nasal, itself. Examples of this are shown for alveolar and bilabial consonants.

N + *Velar* = ŋ

N + kwan	→ ŋ̀kwáń	'soup'
N + go	→ ŋ̀gó	'oil'
N + nwoma	→ ŋ̀nwómá	'a hide / a book'

N + *Alveolar* = n

N + toma	→ ǹtòmá	'cloth'
N + duane	→ ǹdùàné (→ ǹnùàné)	'kinds of food'

N + *Labiodental* = ɱ

N + fasoɔ	→ ɱ̀fàsòɔ́	'profit'
N + frama	→ ɱ̀fràmá	'air'

N + *Bilabial* = m

N + paboa	→ m̀pàbòá	'footwear'
N + boa	→ m̀bóá (→ m̀móá)	'animals'

Number

By number, we mean how the singular and the plural noun forms are formed in Twi. Almost all Twi nouns have prefixes in their singular forms. In fact, as shown here, the Twi vowels can be prefixes in the singular form, except /i, ɪ, u, ʊ/. In the formation of the plurals, however, only one of the vowels, /a/, is sometimes used. The most common plural prefix is the nasal, *N*. As noted, the phonetic form of *N* prefix is dependent on the following consonant in the stem; hence it's diverse representation, demonstrated here:

Singular		Plural		
àdùàné	'food'	→ ǹnùàné	'kinds of food'
àsɛ́m̀	'story'	→ ǹsɛ́m̀	'stories'
òkúsíé	'rat'	→ ŋ̀kúsíé	'rats'
ɔ̀pétɛ́	'vulture'	→ m̀pétɛ́	'vultures'
ɛ̀sɛ́m̀	'bowl'	→ àsɛ́ń	'bowls'
ɔ̀sónó	'elephant'	→ àsónó	'elephants'

A.3 The verb – *àdèyɔ́ ásɛ́m̀ (áhórɔ̀ɔ́)*

Verb in the affirmative form – *Àdèyɔ́ ásɛ́m̀ áhórɔ̀ɔ́ wɔ́ àáné kábèà mú*

By verb forms, we mean the various expressions of a verb with regards to Tense and or Aspect. Twi is considered to have Aspect (not Tense). Basically, there are seven (7) aspectual forms of the verb in Twi. These are i) Imperative, ii) Habitual, iii) Stative, iv) Past, v) Perfect, vi) Progressive, and vii) Future.

In the following, the expression of each of the seven aspectual forms is shown with the verbs, *da* 'to sleep or to lie down' and *gyina* 'to stand or to stop'. Each of the forms is also shown with the subject, *Kofi* 'personal name' and *me* 'the 1st person singular pronoun' (see III above for the various pronouns in Twi) where appropriate.

The imperative form

The imperative form is basically the bare form of a verb. An imperative form of a verb is used to give command. As in the examples below, an imperative form of a verb is normally used without addressee identification.

Twi	English	Twi	English
Dá.	'Sleep.'	Gyìnà.	'Stop.'
Dá hɔ́.	'Sleep there.'	Gyìnà hɔ́.	'Stop/stand there.'
Kɔ̀dá.	'Go to bed.'	Kɔ̀gyìná.	'Go and stop.'

The habitual form

The habitual form of the verb is used to express an activity, action or event that is done regularly; that is, an expression of a routine activity, action or event. For example:

Twi	English	Twi	English
Kòfídá.	'Kofi sleeps.'	Kòfí gyìná.	'Kofi stops.'
Mè dá.	'I sleep.'	Mègyìná.	'I stop.'

The stative form

The stative form, also called continuative, expresses a persistent state or action. In fact, only a few verbs can be used in the stative. For example:

Twi	English
Kòfí dà hó.	'Kofi is lying there.'
Mèdà hó.	'I'm lying down.'
Kòfí gyìnà hó.	'Kofi is standing there.'
Mègyìnà hó.	'I'm standing there.'

The past form

The past form of the verb expresses a single event, having a beginning and an end. It is identified by the suffix, /-e/. This suffix has two surface realizations. As in the examples below, the suffix remains as [-e] when nothing is following the verb. It is, however, realized as a copy of the final vowel in the verb if the verb is followed by another word; i.e., final vowel lengthening in the verb.

Twi	English	Twi	English
Kòfí dà-è.	'Kofi slept.'	Kòfí dà-à hó.	'Kofi slept there.'
Mè dà-è.	'I slept.'	Mè dà-à hó.	'I slept there.'
Kòfí gyìná-è.	'Kofi stopped.'	Kòfí gyìná-à hó.	'Kofi stopped there.'
Mè gyìná-è.	'I stopped.'	Mè gyìná hó.	'I stopped there.'

The perfect form

The perfect form of the verb also expresses an action that has a continuing present relevance of a past situation. It is represented by the prefix /a-/, as shown in the examples below.

Twi	English	Twi	English
Kòfí á-!dá.	'Kofi has slept.'	Kòfí á-!gyíná.	'Kofi has stopped.'
M-à-dá.	'I have slept.'	M-à-gyíná.	'I have stopped.'

The progressive form

The progressive form of the verb expresses an on-going event or an action that is spread over a period of time. It is identified by the prefix /re-/, as shown in the examples below. In pronunciation, the [r] in /re-/ is normally deleted in which case the vowel, [e], is pronounced as the final vowel in the preceding word.

Twi		English
Kòfí rè-dá.	→ Kòfí è-dá.	'Kofi is sleeping.'
Mè-rè-dá.	→ Mè-è-dá.	'I'm sleeping.'
Kòfí rè-gyìná.	→ Kòfí è-gyìná.	'Kofi is stopping.'
Mè-rè-gyìná.	→ Mè-è-gyìná.	'I'm stopping.'

The future form

The future form of the verb expresses an event or an action that is expected to take place at a later date. Two future forms of the verb are distinguished in Twi: Future I and Future II. With Future I, a definite time for an action to take place is not expressed. On the other hand, with Future II, a definite time of immediate future is indicated through the expression, '... is about to'. Future I is identified by the monosyllabic prefix, /bɛ–/ (or be–)/. Future II is identified by the disyllabic prefix /rebɛ– (or rebe–)/, as shown in the examples below.

Future I

Twi	English		Twi	English
Kòfí bɛ́-dá.	'Kofi will sleep.'		Kòfí bé-gyíná.	'Kofi will stop.'
M-ɛ́-dá.	'I'll sleep.'		M-è-!gyíná.	'I will stop.'

Future II

Twi	English
Kòfí (r)ìbɛ̀dá.	'Kofi is about to sleep.' or 'Kofi is about to sleep.'
Mè-(r)èbɛ̀dá.	'I'm about to sleep.' or 'I'm coming to sleep.'
Kòfí (r)ìbɛ̀gy''iná.	'Kofi is about to stop.' or 'Kofi is coming to stop.'
Mè-(r)èbɛ̀gy''iná.	'I'm about to stop.' or 'I'm coming to stop.'

In the negative – *Wɔ̀ dààbí kàbèà mú*

Negation is expressed in the verb in Twi. By negation, we mean how the opposite of an action expressed by an affirmative verb is expressed. In the expression of negation, a nasal prefix or infix, depending on the aspectual form of the verb, is attached to the affirmative form of the verb. As shown before, the phonetic form of the nasal prefix, *N*, is dependent on the following consonant in the verb stem. Examples are shown below.[2]

	Affirmative	Negative		
Imperative	Dá.	→ Ǹdá	→ Ǹná.	'Don't sleep.'
	Gyìnà.	→ Ǹgyiná	→ Ǹŋyìná.	'Don't stop.'
Habitual	Mè dá.	→ Mè ǹdá	→ Mèǹná.	'I don't sleep.'
	Mè gyìná.	→ Mè ǹgyìná	→ Mèǹŋyìná.	'I don't stop.'
Stative	Mè dá hɔ́.	→ Mè ǹdá hɔ́	→ Mèǹná hɔ́.	'I'm not lying there.'
	Mè gyìnà hɔ́.	→ Mè ǹgyìná hɔ́	→ Mèǹŋyìná hɔ́.	'I'm not standing there.'
Past	Mè dá-è.	→ Mè à-ǹdá	→ Mèàǹná.	'I did not sleep.'
	Mè gyìná'e.	→ Mè à-ǹgyìná	→ Mèǹŋyìná.	'I did not stop.'

---

[2] You might notice that the *Past* tense suffix, in isolation, resembles the *Perfect* tense in context, and the *Perfect* tense prefix, in isolation, resembles the *Past* tense in context. This is one of the oddities about Akan-Twi verb forms.

Perfect	M-à-dá.	→ Mè ǹdá-è	→ Mèǹná-è.	'I have not slept.'
	M-à-gyíná.	→ Mè ǹgyìná-è	→ Mèǹŋyìná-è.	'I have not stopped.'
Progressive	Mè-è-dá.	→ Mé-è-ǹdá	→ Méèǹná.	'I'm not sleeping.'
	Mè-è-gyìná.	→ Mé-è-ǹgyìná	→ Méèǹŋyìná.	'I'm not stopping.'
Future I	M-έ-dá.	→ Mé-ǹdá	→ Méǹná.	'I will not sleep.'
	M-é-!gyíná.	→ M-é-ǹgyìná	→ Mé-ǹŋyìná.	'I will not stop.'
Future II	Mè-è-bὲdá.	→ Mé-ǹbὲdá	→ Méémmὲdá.	'I'm not coming to sleep.'
	Mè-è-bègyìná.	→ Mé-ǹbègyìná	→ Mémmègyìná.	'I'm not coming to stop.'

A.4   The adjective – *èdíń áhyέǹsòdéὲ*

In Akan-Twi, an adjective follows the noun it modifies, unlike in English. Where two or more adjectives are modifying a noun, again, unlike in English, the adjectives need not follow any particular pattern. Observe examples in the following.

	Twi	English
Noun	*Adjective*	
àkwàdàà	+ kétéwá	'a small child'
ɔbáá	+ kɔ́kɔ́ɔ́	'a fair lady'
pànìǹ	+ bɔ́né	'a bad or an irresponsible adult'
òdwáń	+ kὲséὲ	'a big sheep'
òdwáń	+ kὲséὲ tùǹtùḿ	'a big black sheep'
òdwáń	+ tùǹtùḿ kὲséὲ	'a big black sheep'
ɔbáá	+ kɔ́kɔ́ɔ́ téátéá fὲὲfé	'a slim fair beautiful lady'
ɔbáá	+ téátéá kɔ́kɔ́ɔ́ fὲὲfé	'a slim fair beautiful lady'
àbàá	+ téńtéń fítáá	'a long white stick'
èdáń	+ fítáá téńtéń	'a long white house'

A.5   The adverb – *àdèyɔ́ ásɛ́ḿ bóáfóɔ́*

Adverbs only come after the verbs or verb phrases they qualify in Twi. This is unlike in English where an adverb may come before or after the verb. Examples of adverbs occurrence with verbs are shown below.

	Twi	*English*
Noun	*Adjective*	
Tènàsè	díńń	'Sit down quietly.'
Fòrò	ǹtɛ́ḿ (só)	'Climb quickly.'
Nàntè	àhókyɛ́rɛ́ só/mú	'Walk majestically.'
Bìsà nò	àbòtérɛ́ só/mú	'Ask (for) her/him patiently.'
Twè	yíé	'Discipline her/him well.'
Kòfí	bɾɛ̀òẁ	'Kofi speaks slowly.'
Ɔ̀báá nó sàà	fɛ́ só	'The lady danced beautifully.'

A.6   Exercises:

1. Memorize the ten vowels in Akan-Twi and list them aloud without looking at the book or your notes.

2. Following your tutor or teacher, pronounce all the vowels in isolation (by themselves), in the context of individual words, and in the context of common phrases. Which are the more difficult vowels for you? Focus on those saying vowels as they occur in some of the most common words and phrases of Akan-Twi (see Chapter 1).

3. Pronounce and write five words with only advanced vowels and another five words with only unadvanced vowels in Twi, *e.g.*:

	Advanced	Unadvanced
i.	ɑfuo	dadɪɛ
ii.	_____	_____
iii.	_____	_____
iv.	_____	_____

4. How many forms can the nasal prefix, *N*, become? Give examples (other than those given to you, here) for each of the various occurrences.

5. Write the singular or the plural counterpart of the following nouns.

Singular		Plural	
i. òdwáń	'sheep'	→ _____ _____	
ii. _____ _____		← m̀fìdíé	'traps'
iii. bépɔ́	'mountain'	→ _____ _____	
iv. _____ _____		← ǹkànéá	'lights'
v. ɔ̀bɔ̀fóɔ́	'hunter'	→ _____ _____	

6. Give the past, progressive, and the future (I) forms of the following verbs in Twi with you as the subject.

		Past	Progressive	Future I
a.	sòmà 'to send'	_____	_____	_____
b.	pìà 'to push'	_____	_____	_____
c.	sú 'to cry'	_____	_____	_____
d.	séné 'to sharpen'	_____	_____	_____

7. Change the following affirmative sentences into negative statements.

    a.   Kòfí dìdí.   'Kofi eats.'

    _____   'Kofi does not eat.'
    b.   Bràbédí.   'Come and eat.'

    _____   'Don't come and eat.'
    c.   Fr̀ɛ̀ pàpá nó má mè.   'Call the man for me.'

    _____   'Don't call father for me.'
    d.   Kòfí ábá kɔ́.   'Kofi has come and gone.'

    _____   'Kofi hasn't come and gone.'

Appendix B

Idiomatic and common expressions – *Àkàsàkòá né dáádáá Ǹsɛ̀m̀bìsá bí*

	Twi	*English*
1	Màyɛ́ àsó.	I'm all ears / I've made ears.
	Mèrètìé páá.	(I'm listening attentively.)
2	ǹkùràtɛ́	keeping watch for mice (pretending to be asleep)
	E.g., Mèrètɛ́ ǹkùrá.	*E.g., I'm pretending to be asleep.*
3	Mèǹhú nè tí ànáá nè dúà.	I can't see its head or tail / I can't make heads or tails of it.
		(total lack of understanding; finding something confusing.)
4	mògyàsɛ́m̀	bloody issue (a serious matter)
	E.g., Àyɛ́ mògyàsɛ́m̀.	*E.g., It has become a serious matter.*
5	twà só	to cut short (to stop something)
	E.g., Twà máńsóń nó só.	*E.g., Stop the litigation.*
6	Kà w'àkómà tó wò yɛ́m̀.	Keep your heart in your stomach.
		(Be patient.)
7	béń	to be well-cooked (to be intelligent)
	E.g., Yàẁ àbéń.	*E.g., Yaw is intelligent.*
8	Fìrì m'àní só.	Get off my eye/face.
		(Go away / Get out of here.)
9	Èfírí tí kɔ̀sí náńsóá.	from head to toe
	E.g., Èfírí tí kɔ̀sí náńsóá nyìnáá yɛ́ nò yá.	*E.g., She/he has pains at very part of her/his body.*
10	Tò ànó mú túó.	to shoot in the mouth (to swear or take an oath; to promise)
	E.g., Àtà átò n'ànó mú túó sɛ́ ɔ̀bɛ́bá.	*E.g., Attah has sworn that he will come.*
11	Tò mú ńkyéné.	to put in salt (to worsen a situation)
	E.g., Àdú átò àsɛ́m̀ nó mú ńkyéné.	*E.g., Adu has worsened the case.*
12	Sì só bíó.	to pound/step on it again (to repeat)

	E.g., Ámá ásì àsɛ́ḿ nó só bíó.	*E.g., Ama has repeated the story.*
13	Twà wò yáḿ.	Cut/slash your stomach. (Go and die. / Go hell.) (A very strong insult!)
14	Tì wò náń ákyí.	Scratch your heels. (Travel.)
	E.g., Kòfí átì nò náń ákyí.	*E.g., Kofi has travelled.*
15	Twì n'àníḿ.	scratch his/her face (to scold / to rebuke)
	E.g., Yàẁ àtwí àbɔ̀fŕá nó áníḿ.	*E.g., Yaw has scolded the child.*
16	Mànyá mètí ádídí.	I've got off with my head. (I've escaped unscathed.)
17	Ɛ̀dà wò hwéné ánó.	It's before your nose. (It's right in front of you.)
18	Ɛ̀wɔ̀ mè ǹsá ánó.	It is at my fingertips. (I'm very good at it.)
	E.g., Sàǹkùbɔ́ wɔ̀ mè ǹsá ánó.	*E.g., Organ playing is at my finger tips.*
19	Fà wò náń sí fáḿ.	Put your foot on the ground. (Assert your authority.)
20	Mè náń sì bìrìbí só.	My foot is on something. (I've something to lean on/live on.)
21	Mà wò náń só.	Lift up your foot. (Hurry up.)
22	Yà àkómá.	Have a heart. (Be patient.)
	E.g., Yàẁ wɔ̀ àkòmà páá.	*E.g., Yaw is very patient.*
23	Ǹté ńtàsúó.	Don't spit. (Don't say anything.)
24	Mègyìnà ǹkwá né òwúó ńkwáńtá.	I'm standing between life and death / I'm involved in a matter of life and death. (I'm in a serious situation.)
25	Fà w'ànó twítwìrì fáḿ.	Drag your mouth on the floor. (Take back what you've said.)
26	dɔ̀ ànàdwò	to farm in the night (to be impotent)
27	Ɔ̀gyè dààmá tù sérɛ́.	He/she weeds for a dime. (He/she has nothing to live on. / He/she is poor.)
28	Ɔ̀àdí ǹkyéné pìì.	He/she has eaten a lot of salt. (He/she is very old.)
29	Màtɔ́ ǹkyéné ákyɛ́.	I've bought salt and given it away. (I've allowed myself to be cheated.)

Appendix C

Some essential euphemisms – *Kàsàkòá áhódóɔ́ bí áà ɛ̀hó híá*

Some offensive words and how to express them inoffensively – *Ǹsɛ̀m̀fí bí né sɛ́nèà yɛ̀ká nò yíé*

Raw		Euphemism	
Twi	**English**	**Twi**	**English**
tìàfí	'toilet'	àgyànáń	'a see off'
dwóńsɔ́	'urine'	ǹsúó	'water'
mògyàgúó	'menstruation'	ǹsábúó	'breaking of hand'
		àfìkyìkɔ́	'going to the backyard'
kɔ̀téɛ́	'penis'	dùà	'tail'
ɛ̀twɛ́	'vagina'	ànáń mú	'between legs'
èdíé	'to have sex'	ǹná	'to sleep (together)'
ɛ̀dáḿ	'madness'	tìrìm̀ká	'a bite in the head'
àkɔ̀m̀fò	'suicide'	dɛ́ḿ; àhòmàsɛ́ń	'harm; rope'

Some offensive statements and how to express them inoffensively – *Ǹsɛ̀m̀kèká áfìàfí bí né sɛ́nèà yɛ̀ká nò yíé*

Raw		Euphemism	
Twi	**English**	**Twi**	**English**
Mèrèkɔ́ tìàfí.	'I'm going to toilet'	Mèrèkò gyá mè náń.	'I'm going to see my legs off'
Mèrèdwòǹsɔ́.	'I'm urinating'	Mèrègú ǹsúó.	'I'm pouring water'
Ɔ̀àgú mógyá.	'She has menstruated'	Ɔ̀àbú nè ǹsá.	'She has broken her hand'
		Ɔ̀àkɔ́ àfìkyíré.	'She has gone to the backyard'

125

Mèdí nò.	'I've had sex with her/him'	Mè né nó ádá.	'I've slept with her/him'
Ɔyὲ kròmfóɔ́.	'She/he is a thief'	Nè ǹsá há nò.	'Her/his hand disturbs her/him'
mè kɔ́tὲ	'my penis'	mè dúà	'my tail'
mè twέ	'my vagina'	mè náń mú / ńtέm̀	'between my legs'
Ɔàbɔ́ dáḿ.	'She/he is crazy'	Nè tí mú ká nò.	'Her/his head bites her/him'
Ɔàkyέ àkɔm̀fɔ̀.	'She/he has committed suicide'	Ɔàdí nè hó dέm̀ / Ɔàséǹ nè hó.	'She/he has done harm to herself/himself'

Some words that might be easily mispronounced in a taboo way – Ǹsὲm̀fùá bí á sὲ àmmá yíé ὲbétímí áyέ ǹsὲm̀ fí.

Intended Word		Taboo Word	
Twi	**English**	**Twi**	**English**
nwɔ̀twé	eight	ὲtwέ	vagina
òtwé	antelope	(same)	(same)
àbátwέ	elbow	(same)	(same)
twὲdéέ	blow	(same)	(same)
kɔ̀kɔ̀té	boar	mè kɔ́tὲ	penis

Appendix D

Àdìǹkrá – Symbols of expressions in Akan

The term, *àdìǹkrá*, refers to a set of symbols that represent aphorisms or expressions (examples given below). The word, *àdìǹkrá*, literally means farewell' in Akan-Twi. The symbols relate to counsel that is given to someone who is embarking on a certain feat (or passage) of life, such as getting married, embarking on travel, entering adulthood, etc.

Àdìǹkrá symbols are inspired by creation, man-made objects, proverbs, etc. and constitute a medium of objective and deep-seated socio-cultural knowledge. The symbols continue to increase in number in a reflection of changes in societal thoughts, occurrences and practices.

Symbol	Expression
	Àkòmá ńtóàsòɔ́ (*joined hearts*) Symbol of understanding and agreement: It is a reminder that much could be achieved with one heart.
	Mpàtàpɔ́ (*reconciliatory knot*) Symbol of reconciliation and peacemaking: It is a reminder that conscious effort must be made to maintain friendship.
	Bí ńká bì (*bite not one other*) Symbol of co-existence, peace and harmony: It advises that peace must be aspired to.
	Fìhàǹkrá (*compound of a house*) Symbol of security, unity and the family: It indicates the importance of belonging or family ties. It reminds us that strength lies in unity.

Symbol	Expression

Ɛpá (*handcuffs*)

Symbol of law, order and captivity:
It indicates respect for authority; a reminder that people must abide by the constitution of the land.

Fùǹtùǹfúnèfú dèǹkyɛ̀ǹfúnèfú (*siamese crocodile*)

Symbol of unity in diversity and democracy:
It is a reminder that all of us work towards the common goal (of a community), although we may have differences.

Nyàmé ǹwú nà màwù (*God never dies and so, I will not die*)

Symbol of God's omnipresence and perpetual existence:
It symbolizes the belief that a man's soul never dies, since it rests with everlasting God after death.

Gyé Nyàmé (*except for God*)

Symbol of omnipotence and immortality of God:
It indicates the people's belief in God.

Nyàmé ńtí ... (*Because of God ...*)

Symbol of faith and trust in God:
It symbolizes the belief that God provides for the needs of mankind.

Bòà mè ná mé ḿmóá wó (*Help me for me to help you.*)

Symbol of cooperation and interdependence:
It advises that we need each other for survival.

Wò ǹsá dà mú áà ... (*if your hand is in it ...*)

Symbol of participatory government, pluralism, and democracy:
This calls for the involvement of everyone in nation building.

Sáńkɔ́fá (*go back for it*)

Symbol of attachment to the past:
It advises on the importance of learning from the past. It also reminds us to go back to our roots.

Symbol	Expression
	Ǹkyìǹkyím (*twisting*) Symbol of dynamism and versatility: It underlines the resourcefulness of mankind. It is a reminder that one needs to take initiative.
	Òwúó átwédéɛ́ (*the ladder of death*) Symbol of mortality of man: It is a reminder that death is inevitable and that it is important for mankind to aspire for a worthy soul in the afterlife.
	Màté ásíé (*I have kept what I have heard.*) Symbol of wisdom and prudence: It advises against gossiping. It also advises that one should be circumspect in communication (or with what he/she says).

Appendix E

Word list (Akan-Twi to English) – *ǹsɛ̀ḿfùá bí*

Note: This short glossary aims to aid the reader in learning the content of this textbook, but will not suffice as a stand-alone dictionary. For advanced proficiency in Akan, we recommend referencing one of the sources listed in Appendix F.

A

àbédéɛ́, n. (ɔ̀bédéɛ́, sg.) – females (female)

àbísá, n. – consultation

àbóá, n. – animal

àbùsùàfóɔ́, n. – family members

àbùsùàfóɔ́, n. – family

àdàagyé, n. – a free time

àdóḿ, n. – grace

àdwúmá, n. – work, job, task

àfé, n. (m̀féɛ́, pl.) – year (years)

àfídíé, n. – machine / trap

àfúó, n. – farm

àfììfíí, n. – vetting

àgórɔ́, n. – game

àhúhúró, n. – hot weather

àkèkàakéká, n. – rumours

àkòǹtàbúó, n. – accountability

àkòǹwá, n. – chair, stool

ánkórɛ́ánkórɛ́, n. – individual(s)

àkwáábá, n. – welcome

àkwàdàá, n. – child

àmànèɛ́, n. – message

àmànèdéɛ́ / àmá!néɛ́, n. – a thing sent by errand

ànáá, conj. – or

ànìdàsóɔ́, n. – hope

ànídíé, n. – respect

ànígyéɛ́, n. – happiness

àníwúó, n. – embarrassment

àsɛ̀m̀pá, n. – good news

àsɛ́ḿ, n. – news, story

àsá, n. – dancing

àsèdá, n. – thanks

àséɛ́, prep. – under

àsɔ́, n. – hoe

àsòm̀dwòéɛ́, n. – peace

àtéḿ, n. – insult

àtènè, n. (tènè, v.) – discipline

àtìrìmùɔ̀déń, n. – wickedness

àwèrɛ́fíré, n. – forgetfulness

B

bàabí, adv. – somewhere

bàakóyɛ́, n. – togetherness

báyíé, n. – witchcraft

báyífóɔ́, n. – witch

báàsè / bɔ́ɔ̀sò, n. – bus

bèsé, n. – cola-nut

bìdíé, n. – charcoal

bíó, n. – again

bòà, v. – to help

bɔ̀kɔ̀ɔ́, n. – slowly

bɔ́, v. – to hit; to kick

bɔ́ń, n. – hole

bɔné, n. – bad

bɔnèfákyɛ́, n. – forgiveness

bɛ̀rɛ̀ɛ̀, n. – slowly

cheat

led person

' bell

leep
nent

veed

ce
away
a shower

own
k

t (yams)

s, market

ause, since
id
f something)

tone
nt. pro. – what
of
useless

ɛhɔ́, adv. – there
ɛhyéɛ́, n. – border
ɛká, n. – a loss
ɛpò, n. – sea
ɛsɛ́n, n. – cooking-ware
ɛwóɔ́, n. – honey

F

fɛ̀ɛ̀fé, adj. – beautiful
fɛ̀ɛ̀féɛ́fɛ́, adv. – beautifully
féréɛ́, n. – shyness
fɛ́m̀, v. – shyness
fá, v. – to take
fàtà, v. – to suit, fit
fé, v. – to vomit; to suck
fìifìi, v. – to vet
fóró, v. – to climb; to get on
frà, v. – to mix
frànkàá, n. – flag

G

gààré, n. – gari (kind of cereal)
géráá, n. – barrel, drum
gó, v. – to soften
góró, v. – to play
gú, v. – to spread

Gy

gyàè, v. – to stop
gyá, v. – to leave behind
gyèéné, n. – onion
gyé, v. – to take
gyé sɛ̀, conj. – except
gyé dí, v. – to believe
gyédíé, n. – belief
gyìmî, n. – stupid

H

há, v. – to hunt
háń, n. – light
hìnì, v. – to open, unlock
hòmè, v. – to breathe; to relax
hó / hònám̀, n. – body
hùnù, v. – to know; to see
hú, v. – to blow

Hw

hwέ, v. – to look

hwáń, int. pro. – who

hwàm̀, n. – a nice smell

hwìè, v. – to pour

hwèhwὲ, v. – to search

hwèrὲmá, n. – whistling

Hy

hyὲdà, v. – to pretend

hyέ, v. – to wear; to score

hyé, v. – to burn

hyìà, v. – to meet

hyìrὲǹ, v. – to brighten

K

kàkŕá, n. – a little, a few

kákrà, n. – the youngest of twins

kànéá, n. – light

kàsà, v. – to talk

kásá, n. – a talk, language

ká ... bóm̀, v. – to combine, add up

ká, v. – to bite; to say

káń, v. – to count

kòà, v. – to bend

kóńtóm̀pó, n. – lie

kòrà, v. – to keep; to repair

kòtókó, n. – porcupine

kúm̀, v. – to kill

kùró, n. – town / city

Ky

kyé, v. – to share; to donate

kyèà, v. – to greet

kyèkyèrè, v. – to wrap; to tie

kyèré, v. – to show; to teach

kyé, v. – to catch, arrest; to fry

kyém̀, v. – to push, in child birth

kyí, v. – to forbid

kyìà, v. – to bend; to greet

kyìnéέ, n. – umbrella

Kw

kwà , n. – nothing

kwákwá, v. – to penalize

kwàámè, p.n. – Kwaame

kwáéέ, n. – forest

L

lὲbέὲ, adj. – stupid

lέέm̀, adj. – quiet, reserve

M

mɔdéń , v. – to do well

má, v. – to give

mààmé, n. – mother, wom

mànè, v. – to send; to turn

màǹfrání, n. – foreigner

mé, pro. (1sg.) – I

m̀má, n. – seeds, children

mó, pro. (2pl.) – you

mónó, adj. – new

m̀páéέ, n. – prayer

m̀pòànó, n. – coast

mùnà, v. – to squeeze (ones

mú, prep. – inside, within

N

nànè, v. – to melt

nàná, n. – grandparent, chie

nàǹté, v. – to walk

nòà, v. – to cook

nìm̀, v. – to know

nú, v. – to stir; to tickle

ǹkɔmmɔ́, n. – conversation

ǹkòǹwá, n. pl. (àkòǹwá,sg.)

ǹnέ, n. – today

ǹnórá, n. – yesterday

nóhwàá, adj. – faraway, rem

nòkwáré, n. – truth

nóm̀, v. – to drink

ǹkábóm̀, n. – union, together

ǹkwá, n. – life

ǹkr̀á, n. – message

ǹkùním̀, n. – victory

ǹsìsóɔ́, n. – appeal

ǹsὲm̀mìsá, n. – questioning,

ǹtórɔ́, n. – lie

ǹtórɔ́twá, n. – act of lying

Ny

nyàǹ, n. – eyesore
Nyàmé, n. – God
nyámàá, n. – a personal name
nyìǹsèǹ, v. – to be pregnant
nyíńséń, n. – pregnancy
nyìnáá, adj. / pro. – all
nyìnàsòó, n. – reason / grounds

Nw

nwéné, v. – to weave
nwíí, n. – hair
nwònò, adj. – bitter
nwóḿ, n. – music
nwùnù, n. – cold

O

òbí, dem. pro. – someone
òbíárá, pro. – everyone
òdwáń, n. – sheep
ògógóró, n. – a kind of alcoholic
ònùá, n. – sibling
Òpènímáá, n. – January
òpúró, n. – squirrel

Ɔ

ɔbɔfóɔ, n. – hunter
ɔdɔ, n. – love
ɔhéné, n. – chief, king
ɔsòáfóɔ, n. – minister, caretaker
ɔsónó, n. – elephant
ɔsɔfó, n. – priest

P

pέ, v. – to like
pàá, n. – labour
pààdíé, n. – labouring
pànyíń, n. – elder
pápá, n. – goodness
pàtà, v. – to compensate, pacify
pìà, v. – to push
pòtɔ, v. – to grind
pòmà, v. – to fix
póń, v. – to close

S

prà, v. – to sweep

sàfòá, n. – key
sámáń, n. – ghost
sàmàǹ, v. – to sue
sá, v. – to dance
sáń, v. – to return
sìè, v. – to bury; to hide
sìká, n. – money, gold
sìkàkókɔ́ɔ, n. – gold
sìsì, v. – to cheat
sì só, v. – to appeal
sŕáà, n. – army, military
sú, v. – to cry
sònè, v. – to sieve
sònèέ, n. – sieve
sóhwέ, v. – to try
sɔré, v. – to wake up; to stand up
sɔrè, v. – to worship
sùàhúnú, n. – knowledge
sùkyèrèmá, n. – snow
súkɔ́twèá, n. – frozen rain

T

tàdéέ, n. – lake
táḿ, v. – to lift
té, v. – to pluck
té, v. – to live at
tèà mú, v. – to shout
tènàsè, v. – to sit down
tírínkwá, n. – luck
tòá, n. – bottle
tó, v. – to throw
tùà, v. – to pay
tú, v. – to dig; to uproot
tùmì, aux. v. – can; to be able
túmí, n. – authority, ability

Tw

twέń, v. – to wait
twá, v. – to cut
twèrè, v. – to write
twéné, n. – bridge
twí, v. – to drive; to grind

W

wɔ, aux. v. – to be; to have

wàrè, v. – to marry

wá, n. – cough

wèà, v. – to crawl

wé, v. – to chew

wòsò, v. – to shake

wó, pro. (2sg.) – you

wó, v. – to give birth

wú, v. – to die

wɔ́má, n. – pestle

Y

yɛ́, v. – to do; to be fine

yá, pro. (1pl.) – we / us

yá, v. – to get

yàákɔ, adj. – sorry

yàréɛ́, n. – sickness

Yàá, p.n. – Yaa (a female name)

yáá, n. – pain(s)

yààdíé, n. – mourning

yáḿ, v. – to grind

yàréɛ́, n. – sickness

yàréfóɔ́, n. – sick person

yí, v. – to cut (hair); to trap

yìwáḿ, n. – razor

yíé, adv. – well

yómá, n. – camel

Appendix F

References / Resources for Learning Twi

1. Arthur, G.F.K. 2001. *Cloth as Metaphor: (Re)reading the Adinkra Cloth Symbols of the Akan of Ghana.* Accra: Centre for Indigenous Knowledge Systems.
2. Berry, J., and A. A. Aidoo. 1975. *An Introduction to Akan.* Evanston, IL.: Northwestern University. Pp. 336.
3. Bureau of Ghana Languages. 1975. *Language Guide (Asante Twi)*, 5th ed.
4. Denteh, A. C. 1974. *Spoken Twi (Asante) for Non-Twi Beginners.* Accra-North: Pointer Limited. Pp. 68.
5. Dolphyne, F.A. 1996. *A comprehensive course in Twi (Asante) for the non-Twi learner.* Ghana Universities Press. Book no.: HKULIB 496.338582421 D6.
6. Kotey, P.A. 1998. *Twi-English, English-Twi Dictionary.* Hippocrene Books INC, 0781802644.
7. Kotey, P.A. 2001. *Lets Learn Twi - Ma Yensua Twi.* African World Press, 0865438544.
8. Rapp, E. L. 1936. *An Introduction to Twi, Twi ne Engiresi kasa nhyemmu.* London: Longmans, Green and Co.
9. Redden, J. E. *et al.* 1963. *Twi Basic Course.* Washington, D.C.: Foreign Service Institute, U.S. Department of State. (with tapes).
10. Stewart, J. M. 1969. *Drills for the Indicative Active Tenses of the Asante Verb.* Legon: Institute of African Studies, University of Ghana.